The Ballarat gold rush of the 1850's lives again at Sovereign Hill.

Victoria
with love

Victoria with love

Some personal views of life in Victoria, Australia

Editor: Gina O'Donoghue

Editorial assistance: Rod Nicholls, Robin
Campbell-Berry.
Publicity Unit, Department of the Premier,
Victoria.

ISBN 0 7241 8243 8   Paper case bound
ISBN 0 7241 8246 2   Cloth case bound
ISBN 0 7241 8239 X   Leather bound

F.D. Atkinson, Government Printer,
Melbourne.

Design: Cunningham/Cummings and
Associates, Melbourne.

This book is typeset in Memphis Light by
Meredith Trade Lino and printed on
Ballarat Grenville Dull Art 135 gsm.
Colour separations and plates: Enticott/
Polygraph

Acknowledgements:
Sheep photo page 100 courtesy
Australian Wool Corporation;
Wool fashion photo page 100 courtesy
Tullo by Fletcher Jones;
ANZ Bank photo by Rennie Ellis page 91,
courtesy of Australian Business magazine;
Highland band photo page 131
courtesy Free Entertainment In the Parks.
Olivia Newton-John photo page 9 by
Herb Ritz.

Contents

What sort of place is Victoria?

A land of tropic blue skies and endless summers? Not always. Where people are as numerous as the grains of sand? Certainly not.

What, then?

Well . . . here's another view. Victoria — where interesting things are, like the horizon, limited only by the time available for exploration. Where, after the fashion of the weather, people tend to be warm and pleasant, often surprising, never to be underestimated.

Alternatively . . .
This book presents you with 14 other views of Victoria. All are very different, all have a personal perspective.

Victoria, with love.

This is not a Travel Guide: it's a visit home.

Victoria with love

by Olivia Newton-John

Victoria is still "home" to Olivia Newton-John, although these days she lives mainly in Los Angeles. "People always think me a little strange," she says, "when I tell them that roaring lions remind me of Melbourne."

What can I tell you about Victoria? When I was asked to write this I was a bit apprehensive, as I am a novice at getting my thoughts down on paper. And anyway how can I describe home? There is so much to say, I'm sure to forget something; but here goes —

Well, first of all, I grew up in Melbourne after moving there from England with my family. I was only five years old but I still remember my first impressions on arriving — the city's old world charm, the English trees, old buildings, clean air and sunshine, its wide open spaces — parks and gardens, mountains and marvellous beaches. I didn't realize until I had the opportunity to travel overseas, just how fortunate I was to have grown up with this great sense of space and freedom in such an unspoiled environment. It was during these travels that I realized how lucky I had been and how much I had taken these things for granted.

Australians tend to think of Victoria as a small place, because it is the smallest State on the mainland; and yet in world terms, it's not small at all. It's as big as England, which has over 46 million people, or California, which has nearly 23 million. Yet Victoria's population is only about four million, so there's plenty of room. Most of the people live in the cities, and that means that when you want to get away by yourself, there's lots and lots of places to do it. It's really a lovely combination — you can stay in Melbourne, which is a very sophisticated place now, or you can head off into the bush and be quite alone.

Many of my fondest memories of growing up in Victoria are of the times my family spent just enjoying the good things in nature. We'd go camping to one of my favourite places, Mallacoota — on the eastern coast about 540 kilometres from Melbourne — where we used to camp above the lagoon. I think that the Victorian coastline is magnificent. I especially like the Great Ocean Road which clings to the surf for 200 kilometres from the holiday resort of Anglesea to the Port Campbell National Park.

We once camped in a cow field at night, and left the next day for an outing.

Whilst we were gone, there was a violent rain storm; the cows trampled the tent and destroyed everything except cans of condensed milk with cows faces on them!

Speaking of families, that's something I miss very much living so far from home. My family is spread out all over Australia, but my brother and mother still live in Melbourne. I try to go home at least once a year and we always have an outing together, like going to the Dandenongs for a barbecue or to Phillip Island to see the penguins.

Victorians are very family oriented, and this becomes very apparent on special days like Moomba (Victoria's answer to Mardi Gras) held in March, the big Australia Day parade or the Royal Melbourne Show. I can remember collecting "show bags" full of samples of different foods and lollies — I think these are unique to the Melbourne Show, as I have never seen them anywhere else in the world.

Horses were a passion of mine as a child and I really haven't changed. In Australia I could ride a horse for miles and miles on wide clean beaches without ever seeing a soul. I do miss the wide open spaces.

I have quite a menagerie of animals now, but at that time I had to be content with visiting the zoo, which fortunately for me was situated close to my home at the Melbourne University. At night I could hear the sound of lions roaring. The zoo has improved a great deal since then — it now has landscaped garden enclosures and the most extensive zoo educational service for children in the Southern Hemisphere. People always think me a little strange when I tell them that roaring lions remind me of Melbourne.

In the early days of Melbourne, rows and rows of little terrace houses, rather like you can see in New Orleans, were built as inner city dwellings. These Victorian houses went out of favour for a while, but now people are rediscovering them and restoring them to their former beauty, which has brought a great deal of life to the older suburbs. As a teenager I lived in one, in Jolimont, right near the city. I loved that house: it had a lot of character.

I like old things — old houses, old wares and antiques. Antiques are very fashionable now and there are bric-a-brac shops all over the country. Of course, anything over fifty years old seems "antique" in Australia — it's such a young nation.

Entire country towns from the last century have even been restored. Maldon for instance, is about 135 kilometres north of Melbourne, off the Calder Highway. I used to go into the country on riding weekends and places like Maldon had almost been forgotten. But the town has now become a big curiosity shop: you can fossick there for hours, particularly in the Victorian Lace Shop — its walls, floors, tables, every square inch is covered in lace shawls, bed spreads, curtains, table cloths and christening gowns. Some are original Victoria lace pieces, others are made today in the old patterns.

Maldon is one of the signs that Victorians are becoming more aware of their heritage. The State flourished in the early days when gold was discovered, and people rushed to Victoria not only from all over Australia but from all over the world. Great houses were built with the money from gold and wool, and funny little townships sprang up around the gold mines. Now, of course, most of the mines are no longer worked, but the best of them have been preserved not only for educational purposes, but also as tourist attractions. The one that I'm thinking of is Sovereign Hill near Ballarat, a famous re-creation of the 1850's gold town. There is another "colonial" town at Swan Hill on the Murray River. These two places seem to me like "frozen" towns where the people live and work, and go about their "olde worlde" business just as their predecessors did in the 1800s — dressed in period costume. It's like stepping back a hundred years or more.

I love to shop — what girl doesn't? And Melbourne's downtown area certainly offers everything one's heart could desire. Outside the city proper, too, there are some fine antique shops and art galleries. I have spent many an afternoon "window shopping" in boutiques on Chapel Street, Prahran. The clothes are great and one can be assured of a "once-off" design. Near to the city are the elegant suburbs of South Yarra and Toorak. This is where I would go as a school girl and gaze at the beautifully groomed women and dream that maybe one day I would have a home there and buy imported clothes.

Where I spent my time after school and at weekends was at the coffee lounges and delicatessens in the city, Carlton and St. Kilda. There is a true continental flavour there as so many of the locals are from Europe and brought their customs and foods with them. Boy, am I pleased that they did — I love food, and you can find any kind that you can think of in these areas. My idea of heaven was spaghetti and a cappuccino at Pellegrini's, after a long day at school.

We also have a large Chinese community in Melbourne, and the prices at Chinatown, even in the more exclusive places, haven't become outrageous as in London and Paris.

One thing that overseas visitors may not have heard before is the expression "BYO". It stands for Bring Your Own — alcohol, that is. In many restaurants you can bring your own: it's cheaper that way. So if someone says to you "BYO", don't worry, you're not being insulted.

If you prefer to "CYO", Cook Your Own, we have the Victoria Market. It has the greatest atmosphere, and has an infinite variety of fresh foods and vegetables. I remember going there with my Mum and wheeling the food basket for her, and then taking the good old tram home. Victoria is the only State in Australia that still has the tram, and Melbourne wouldn't be the same without it.

There is so much more that I could say, but it could take forever. I am really lucky to have grown up in such a wonderful place, with such down-to-earth and generous people. It gave me a solid foundation for the rest of my life. I may not live there now, but Melbourne is still home to me.

Victoria, with love
Photography by Ron Ryan.

Melbourne's parks, at the centre of the Garden State. Fitzroy Gardens — with its white-walled conservatory and nearby Captain Cook's Cottage, transplanted from England — adjoins Treasury Gardens, a favourite spot for picnickers and jogging Parliamentarians; parklands along the Yarra River; and the Royal Botanic Gardens, where the swans are always hungry.

Wildlife in Victoria —

Unique Penguin Parade at Phillip Island. At dusk, every day of the year, tiny Fairy Penguins emerge from the sea, delighting waiting spectators.

The endearing koala — also to be seen on Phillip Island . . .

. . . The endangered Leadbeater's Possum, Victoria's faunal emblem.

Lyrebirds displaying splendid tails in Sherbrooke Forest.

Stumpy-tailed Lizard, and friend.

Kangaroos feeding at Fraser National Park.

◁
Rhythm of the city —

Melburnian Eliza Doolittle, Bourke Street Mall.

Famous trams, now sometimes orange or custom-painted as well as the traditional yellow-and-green.

Parliament House and St. Patrick's Cathedral, in sunny background; and night on St. Kilda Road, with the illuminated Shrine of Remembrance.

▷
Spectrum of the city, including St. Paul's Cathedral, consecrated 1891; River Yarra bridges with original decorative streetlights; 'art-deco' trams and football crowds; architecture of the office; and Flinders Street railway station's exotic entrance reflected by brass nameplate of Young and Jackson's brassy pub.

(Following page)
City living by night and day —

The "Great Space" at Collins Place, Melbourne's major new hotel, office and shopping complex, includes entertainers as well; lounge area in City Square offers a more restful pace.

Victoria Market, serving fresh food to Melbourne since 1877. Victoria's people come from many countries; all tastes can be catered, not only in food but in entertainment, culture, and religious observance.

Simple grace and charm in older houses
keeps them much in demand.

◁
Gala events — Melbourne Cup day, when a
horse-race stops a nation; the Royal
Agricultural Show; and Moomba Festival in
March, with its cheerful float parade.

▷
The ski season in Victoria lasts June /
September.

Victorians love the sea — not surprising, since there's more than 1200 kilometres of ocean coastline.

<
The past preserved at historic Maldon township — the Victorian Lace Shop, and main street by night.

▷
Victoria's far north —

Paddle steamers still ply the Murray River, their cargo now holiday-makers instead of wheat, sheep and prospectors.

Blacksmith's forge and the Dispensary at Swan Hill Folk Museum — living history for all to witness.

Werribee Park, between Melbourne and Geelong —

Loving and authentic restoration of this magnificent colonial mansion includes the opulent Drawing Room (right) and the very masculine Billiard Room complete with big game trophies.

Victoria's State Equestrian Centre is being developed at Werribee Park. Showjumping will join polo (far left) and polocrosse — already popular events there.

Confessions of a Victorian Gentleman

by Barry Humphries.
Photography by Peter Thomson.

There's another side to Barry Humphries, world traveller and creator of innumerable Music Hall characters. Putting aside the satire for a while, he reflects here on "that leafy, unchanging, immensely comforting world which the citizens of Melbourne can never wait to get home to."

"Whenever I begin to assemble the elements of a new stage play," he adds, "Melbourne is my theme and Victoria my inspiration."

In my youth I aspired to be a landscape painter and ended up a comedian. The former enterprise often provided as much public amusement as my later theatrical adventures. Every school holiday would find me scrambling around the terracotta cliffs of Mornington, where my parents owned a sea-side bungalow, in search of a secluded painting site. Only when the portable easel had been erected and I stood before the empty canvas in my sola topee with its green fly-veil squeezing the first worm of aromatic Windsor and Newton's oil paint onto my palette did my audience start emerging from the bushes. Although a net protected me from the invasion of bright-winged insects there was no protection from those clusters of gaudy holiday-makers who spring from no-where whenever an artist sets up his gear.

Perhaps they are drawn by some mysterious property in the odour of turpentine, for they seem to abandon any plans they might have entertained for their day's recreation in order to slouch and skulk within inches of the unhappy landscapist. Loud is their laughter at your eccentric pastime and invariably forthright is their criticism. As you try to pretend they are not there scrabbling in the dust and knocking over your thermos flask, one of their kiddies will barge up and push his finger through your canvas with the words: "What's that supposed to be, mister?" (Loud laughter from its parents, who have decided to set up a picnic several feet behind you.)

Other artists have told me that they have successfully painted out of doors without the slightest interruption from an inquisitive public, so I can only reflect, all these many years later, that I must have presented a richly comic spectacle. The tragedy of the professional humorist is, however, that he always takes himself too seriously.

In those far-off golden summer days I had a deeply serious desire to record the picturesque aspects of my native State of Victoria, as they had never been depicted before. I had a special love for the beaches around Port Phillip Bay and I knew of no greater pleasure than a day spent perched on a cliff with a loaded paint brush gazing out over the sparkling water. A lot of sea is of course, tremendously useful to the amateur painter because it conveniently fills up so much of the picture. However, I did not confine myself to that wonderfully varied and deliciously picturesque coast between Frankston and Sorrento, but sometimes ventured inland with a few extra tubes of green and ochre to paint the landscape of the Mornington Peninsula. An apple orchard in blossom at Red Hill, a Shoreham homestead, a Dromana hillside, an old-fashioned garden at Baxter.

A few of these youthful daubs have survived, and when I look at them today I can precisely recall the pleasures of those hours spent at the easel: the honeysuckle swarming over the fence of a Mornington vicarage, the scent of sun on pine-needles, and the perfume of the tea-tree amidst which I so often pitched my painting tackle.

In my theatrical career I have attempted another kind of portraiture. My subjects are the people of Melbourne, and in depicting them as truthfully as I can I have none the less sought out in the great mass of ordinary life that which is whimsical, or odd or exceptional in my fellow citizens, just as in my youth I would scour a landscape for its most picturesque or typical aspect. Whenever I return to my native city of Melbourne and begin to assemble the elements of a new stage play it is the 'look' of the characters and the landscapes they inhabit which interest me most. I regard my subjects with a draughtsman's eye, and even if I

am performing in Leeds, or Edinburgh, or
Dublin or Toronto, Melbourne is my
theme and Victoria my inspiration.

I was born in the suburb of Kew and
my earliest recollection of the world was
a Melbourne garden in March.
Honeysuckle, Agapanthus, Belladonna
lilies and perhaps the livid glow of a few
Cannas bloomed over my bassinet.

Those earliest impressions of nodding
colour and sun-dappled shrubbery,
fragrant lawns and rainbow sprinklers
still exert upon me the most potent of
spells, so that today I can re-experience
an infantile joy merely by strolling on an
idle Sunday afternoon through the leafy
suburbs of Melbourne.

At no other time in the year,
however, do I miss my home town more
than in late April when the city basks in
what must surely be the finest autumn
climate in the world. The tragedy which
has in recent times robbed England of its
venerable population of Elm trees has
not, mercifully, overtaken Victoria and
these trees can be seen in their fullest
glory in the Fitzroy and Treasury gardens
in the city's heart. As April enters May
they turn from gamboge to old gold, and
in the sharper evening air are wafted the
evocative odours of leaf mould and the
acrid sweetness of suburban bonfires.

How powerfully such a composite
smell as this — an olfactory chord as it
were — quickens the heart and speaks to
us urgently out of the past!

One of the happiest holidays of my
youth was spent in the Dandenong
Ranges in the smoky, mulch-scented
month of May. The house we had rented
lay at the end of a long Chestnut avenue
wherein we searched for nuts among the
large tawny leaves. At night we roasted
our haul in the glowing debris of a great
stone fireplace where eucalyptus logs
had blazed all day; and in the damp
green mornings, our breath smoking in
the chill, we took long walks through the
mossy aisles and transepts of Sherbrooke
Forest listening for lyrebirds under the tall
ferns and gigantic trees.

'The Dandies' are still one of
Melbourne's most glorious assets, and
repay a visit at any season. The
Devonshire Tearooms of my childhood,

many fashioned in an entirely appropriate 'Tudor' style, still exist; but one can also find excellent restaurants in these hills today. Though parts of that majestic Mountain Ash forest survive and are protected by the strictest laws, the presence of European trees enriches the more domesticated slopes of the Dandenongs and autumn excursions to view 'the tints' are an imperative ritual to all lovers of the Copper Beech and Liquid Amber.

Another favourite childhood haunt was Wattle Park, a bushland reserve close to our house, which in the month of August is a mass of golden blossoming Acacia. Except that it is now enclosed by suburban streets and gardens whereas it once melted into the landscape of Box Hill, Wattle Park survives today; a pleasant thirty minute tram ride from the City.

But no less evocative than the powdery fragrance of these native Mimosas in glorious bloom is the scent of Pittosporum in flower. A native of Victoria, this evergreen shrub with its small waxen flowers has been trained into hedges in many of Melbourne's older suburbs and in warm spring weather its perfume hangs delectably on the night air.

I remember an evening in late August several years ago when I revisited Melbourne after a long absence. Catatonic with jet-lag I sat in the taxi which carried me from the airport to my parents' home in Camberwell. We stopped at some lights in Hawthorn and I opened the window. A gale of Pittosporum of the most exquisite sweetness and potency enveloped me utterly. It was as though in that one magnificent *whiff* I re-lived all the joyful moments of my youth.

At another time I was in Portugal staying at an hotel which had once been a monastery. One evening after dinner I strolled in a part of the old gardens which had been planted with a variety of exotic trees, and suddenly, on the night air came the inimitable intoxicating fragrance of Pittosporum!

And an instant evocation of Melbourne.

I have so far dwelt on horticultural aspects of my home State to the exclusion of that which interests me especially, and is the chief glory of Victoria: architecture.

The marvellous thing about Australia's capital cities is that they are all so different in character. There is a sinister type of developer and town planner abroad today who seeks to destroy this wonderful architectural variety; who would turn all our cities if he could into collections of forlorn cement boxes.

This monster has left his mark on most modern cities in the world. He sits on planning committees and signs demolition orders. Whenever we see an office block that looks as though it was designed by an accountant we behold one of his victories. Whenever a sound Victorian building is razed to create a car-park we know he has shares in the adjacent supermarket.

He is pursuasive in his arguments. He preaches 'Progress' and promotes doubtful catchphrases like 'quality of life' and 'environmental planning'. We are right to distrust him, because in recent years he has defrauded Australians of a portion of their architectural inheritance. In Melbourne his reign is at an end.

In Melbourne the opulent and optimistic buildings of the past remain to compliment their lofty modern neighbours. More than any city in Australia the Victorian capital has more beautiful buildings than it has ugly ones. Nor are they all to be found in the heart of town. I like the old post office at Flemington with its delicious brick clock tower, tucked away in one of Melbourne's many unspoiled suburban backwaters, so that one only glimpses it from the busy High Street.

I also admire the Witherby tower at Melbourne Grammar School now that its clock no longer summons me to irksome hours of wasted time on the football pitch. Today I can flit like a ghost around my Alma Mater's bluestone gothic revival precinct, or sit on a bench beneath the cloistered facade without being told to get my hair cut by a boy my own age with an undistinguished career ahead of him on the Stock Exchange.

The St Kilda Road is Australia's only boulevard and the best way to see it is from a Melbourne tram. These charming and efficient vehicles are painted cream and green and it is in these traditional hues that citizens prefer to behold them, though festive experiments in alternative coach-painting have from time to time been attempted.

On the left, past Melbourne Grammar School, is a block of flats in the 'moderne' style called Kia Ora. These flats, built in the late 'thirties to house fugitives from totalitarian Europe, are a model of their kind. They have also, in recent years, been impeccably restored to their former 'art deco' elegance.

Apartment buildings are comparatively rare in Melbourne, whose inhabitants prefer to live in their own homes embowered in their own gardens. To be sure we have some splendid balconied terraces in the Italianate style, the finest of which can be seen in South Melbourne, Fitzroy and Clifton Hill, but it is the detached bungalow, in a multitude of stylistic variations, which is most typical of Melbourne.

What a rich field of exploration this city presents to the student of domestic architecture! There are the 'Queen Anne' houses in Armadale and Hawksburn with their asymetrical plan and steep gables crowned with terra cotta gryphons and wyverns. There are the stucco'd and iron lace verandah'd mansions of Hawthorn — whole streets of them — erected in the 1870s on the high ground above the willowed Yarra. Hawthorn, and the older parts of Brighton, are amongst the world's most beautiful suburbs, and the explorer should here scan the horizon for those venerable Norfolk Island pines which invariably signpost an old garden and an even lovelier house.

By contrast I would suggest a visit to North Balwyn where I used to set up my easel and paint the lush gorse-covered hills. This was before that rolling landscape was overwhelmed by the substantial suburban developments which came with the prosperous 'fifties. Chubby new homes like cream brick radiograms squinted out over the raw new crescents, drives and groves through their smug venetian blinds. Today, the houses which seemed so brash and intrusive with their infant lawns, Silver Birches and diminutive Rhodedendrons have mellowed. Fashion has turned its back on Balwyn as Melburnians strive to live closer to town; and the sparse shrubbery of the 'fifties has prospered in that orchard soil, softening the idiom of porch and feature chimney and restoring to Balwyn that sweet sense of landscape one thought had vanished.

The Balwyn of the 'twenties, Camberwell embodies for me the best aspect of Melbourne suburbia. I grew up there and know all its tree-lined streets by heart. I love its houses too, its Californian bungalows, its cream stucco'd Spanish Missions with their barley sugar balconies. Here, set back behind Plane tree, Maple and Privet hedge stand those comfortable monuments to respectability and neighbourly virtue — each different — yet each house a reassuring echo of its stylistic twin a few streets away. In Camberwell neo-Tudor calls to its half-timbered tapestry brick relative across back fences and tangled Morning Glory. A double-storied Georgian revival sits grandly behind its pedestal bird bath and camellia tree, whilst next door, all manganese brick and corner windows, a nautical looking dwelling of the late 1930s in the style they called 'ultra moderne' still flaunts its festoon blinds, glass bricks, its Daphne, Japonica and ornamental Kumquat.

Look out over any suburban panorama in Melbourne from a convenient hilltop and you will see more trees than houses, more leaves than tiles. The shopping centres change; the 'little man around the corner' gives way to more impersonal 'marketing outlets', but turn off any road in my home town and you will find yourself in that leafy, unchanging, immensely comforting world which the citizens of Melbourne can never wait to get home to.

There is a small railway station on the Ashburton line I especially love, and which I revisited after a quarter of a century. It had barely changed in all those years except that someone had aerosol'd a modish admonition on the fence about Aboriginal land rights.

It was from this charming, almost rural platform that I daily commenced my long journey to school, and in a non-smoking first class compartment of that comfortable mulberry-coloured electric train I accomplished much of my early reading. In the thirty minutes or so that it took to reach Melbourne's splendidly domed Byzantine terminus in Flinders Street, I consumed countless volumes of prose and verse, all bought for no more than a shilling or two from the city's many emporiums of second-hand literature.

The exigencies of modern commerce have obliged these most civilised of shopkeepers to retreat from the centre of town and today browsers and bookworms must pursue their vice in the side streets of older suburbs like Armadale, Glenferrie and Prahran.

But the lover of books and fine architecture should endeavour at all costs to visit one of Australia's most distinguished reading rooms: the library at the Parliament House.

One of the chief glories of this arcane and opulent chamber is the view it commands of Wardell's great cathedral of St Patrick, which must surely stand alongside Pearson's St Peter's in Brisbane as one of the two finest gothic buildings in the Southern Hemisphere. The library windows frame our view of the cathedral in a manner which politely excludes two recent examples of 'brutalist' architecture which have been allowed to flaunt their gross profiles within a few yards of St Patrick's graceful spire.

In the last few years I have resumed two of the more delightful recreations of my youth: painting and cycling. Our town planners have certainly made the latter pastime less of a chore than it once was, and I recommend to the blithe bicyclist a spin along the Yarra's bank from Prince's Bridge to the picnic slopes of Studley Park.

It is little wonder that Victoria has nurtured so many fine painters of landscape, besides myself. One has only to think of Conder's Heidelberg or Buvelot's Mount Martha, Harold Herbert's Lorne and S. T. Gill's Ballarat, Withers' Templestowe and Tom Roberts'

Dandenong. In more recent years Sidney Nolan has commemorated St Kilda and Arthur Boyd Berwick and the Wimmera, John Perceval has painted Williamstown and Mr Brack has given us Collins Street and Dame Edna Everage.

Mention of this famous actress and *diseuse* calls to mind the theatres which have for many years provided Melburnians with a stream of varied entertainment. The Princess, Her Majesty's, the Comedy and the Atheneum remain perennially popular with audiences and artistes alike. The completion of the Victorian Arts Centre complex will do much to augment the city's traditionally rich theatrical life.

Whenever I return to Melbourne by 'plane, I am more than ever pursuaded that the drive from the Tullamarine aerodrome into town is finer than any other I know. The highways which conduct travellers to and from airports are usually grim affairs flanked by tanneries and hovels, factories and refuse dumps. Not so in Melbourne where the visitor or returning resident is conducted from the tarmac through a green and expansive pastoral landscape past garden suburbs and thence swiftly to the city's commercial heart.

If the population of Melbourne has a conspicuous fault, it is an indifference to one great natural advantage: the water. Melbourne's drinking water is of a quality and sweetness which would elsewhere be bottled. If I were to now propose a loyal toast to this my native State of Victoria, it would be with a brimming beaker of this incomparable and hyaline beverage.

Fun and games and civilization

by Ron Clarke

In 1956, a striking 19-year-old youth wearing Australia's green-and-gold proudly carried the torch which ignited the Olympic flame. The youth, Ron Clarke, went on to become Victoria's greatest athlete: and later, a successful Melbourne businessman. In this article, he looks at sport and leisure, participation and pleasure, in Victoria — a place, he says, in which to live the good life.

I like to run. For me, it's not just a hobby — and it's more than a sport: it's a state of being.

Counting up, I've realised that I must have run something like twenty thousand miles around Melbourne, through most of her parks and along every track. I've trained on the streets in the suburbs, sprinted through the city, and trekked across Australia's biggest bridge — West Gate.

I know Melbourne the way only a runner can — I've thrown away the road maps and made my own routes.

My running has taken me to 40 or 50 different countries — not just as a tourist, but as a competitive athlete. When you compete in another country or another climate you get hold of the feel of the place and identify the differences which make it unique.

What do I look for in a place? Natural beauty, of course. Good air to breathe. And a perfect place to run. These are the things that mean most to me, and if Victoria didn't fill each of these bills, I wouldn't be here.

I have a passion for health and recreation, and for nearly all sports. If I haven't played them I've become an enthusiastic spectator, and I'm clearly aware that there are few places on this earth that can match the facilities we have for sport and recreation in Victoria.

Look at the M.C.G. — the Melbourne Cricket Ground. It's been there since 1853, since just after Melbourne itself. "A good place for a village", said Batman — and, he, or a bowler, could have added, "a place to play cricket". The M.C.G. — always locally referred to just like that, em-see-gee — is mentioned all over the world when conversation turns to great moments in cricket.

All the best have played there — Bradman and Trumper, Hutton and Hall, Lillee, Sobers, the Pollocks, the Bedsers and the marvellous Chappells. On a thousand occasions Victoria's own cricketers have worn the floppy green cap of Australia at the M.C.G.: Cowper, Stackpole, Redpath, "Tangles" Max Walker, and Bill Lawry, "the Phantom"

Over six brilliant summer's days at New Year, 1937, more than 350,000 people paid to watch Australia inflict a definitive defeat on the oldest rival, England — setting a world record for attendance at a cricket match which still stands, after all these years.

The M.C.G. also holds the record for the biggest crowd to come together to watch cricket on a single day: 90,800 people, me amongst them, went through the turnstiles on 11 February, 1961, to watch the Aussies take on cricket's new power, the West Indies. No double centuries from Bradman or McCabe as in '37 — but still another Aussie victory, by a slim two wicket margin, after that great fast bowler Wes Hall was at least partially tamed by one of our best-ever opening pairs, Colin McDonald and Bob Simpson.

Victorians like to compete, and there *is* a devotion to cricket's flannelled fools — but it doesn't even *rate* when you mention "football". Australian Rules Football, organized nationally through the Victorian Football League, has practically reached the heady heights of religion.

Aussie Rules is big! Everything about the game is big — the attention it gets, the tempers it raises, the followers, the crowds, the traffic to and from football grounds — even the oval it's played on is the biggest of all team sports arenas — a minimum 180 metres long and 150 metres wide.

I've never seen action like it and it's got to be seen live to be understood. Eighteen fiercely fit players are in each team and most of the time they're *all* running or jumping or competing for the oval ball. "Footy" is ferocious, it's brilliant and it's exacting.

This insane football game was born on the grounds of the M.C.G. In winter, the cricketers shake their heads in disbelief at the mudpatch which, during summer, is one of the world's most famous cricket pitches.

In a way, the massive crowds of Victorians attending sporting events like football, horse racing, cricket, and tennis — spectators rather than participants — brought to life a unique and wonderful character. His name is Norm. Norm's the lazy side of all of us — relaxing in front of

the telly with a can of beer, freely offering advice to umpires, referees and players at all or any sporting events.

By the end of 1975, the pot bellies of many Norms seemed to signify that Victorians were becoming "watchers" instead of "doers": then the promotional campaign "Life. Be In It" was launched.

"Life. Be In It", put together by the Youth, Sport and Recreation Ministry, and a very talented adman Phillip Adams, got the people of Victoria up and out and participating. The campaign's amazing success has seen its ideas spread nationwide, and across the Pacific to the U.S.

Of course a health and fitness campaign like "Life. Be In It", aimed at every person in Victoria, couldn't have been a success unless the opportunities and the facilities were there in the first place.

As I write on a very pleasant autumn's day, simultaneously there are around 220,000 Australian football players of all ages actually engaged in matches and from 100,000 to 200,000 tennis players involved on the 150,000 tennis courts there are in the State, despite the fact that the summer season has finished. During the week, 70,000 basketball players would have played at least one game of their sport, as have 60,000 soccer players and 170,000 golfers. The season is just finishing for 80,000 lawn bowlers.

This does not count the squash players, the athletes, the badminton players, the yachtsmen out on the Bay, the hockey players and the nigh-on 100,000 netball players who participate in their sport every week.

For me, the heart of Victoria's sporting activities is over the railway lines from the M.C.G.: at Olympic Park. Its athletic track has fond memories for me for it was there that I competed almost every Saturday for twenty years and set my first world records. The Park complex includes, in Victoria's inimitable style and devotion to gambling, a dog racing track; plus what was once the swimming pool of the 1956 Olympics.
Quarter-of-a-century and more than ten million dollars later, the Olympic Pool is

now the site of Victoria's spanking new indoor recreation centre — offering 7,000 seats, all with a perfect view, for rock concerts and ice follies as well as basketball and ice hockey. Tennis, too — providing an indoor venue to rival the superb grass courts of Kooyong, four kilometres away, down the South-Eastern Freeway. Swimming, which is possibly Australia's major sport and pastime, is hardly being neglected. Less than a kilometre from the old pool, through the parklands along Batman Avenue, nearly five million dollars has gone into the Olympic-standard facilities at the State Swimming Centre, based on the historic Beaurepaire Pool.

Also, in the middle of the Olympic running-track is the headquarters of soccer in Victoria. The round-ball game seems to be growing all the time. After a curiously delayed start, soccer's popularity has surged with the creation of a national league, and the coming of soccer-crazy European migrants. Most of them won't even use the term "soccer": "It's football", they say, "played with the feet".

The list of Victoria's sports stars goes on and on: Alan Jones and Geoff Hunt, both champions of the world, in motor-racing and squash respectively. There are the tennis greats: Fraser, Sedgman, Margaret Court, and the new Mac twins — McNamara and MacNamee. Cyclists Sid Paterson and Russell Mockridge, golfer Peter Thomson, Roy Higgins and Bill Williamson from horse-racing: these are all magical names for me.

And, of course, the runners: John Landy, so nearly the first four-minute miler, the dashing Ralph Doubell; and Herb Elliot, who came from the West to train in Victoria: his gold medal in the 1,500 metres at Rome in 1960 came after three years of toiling in the sand dunes of Portsea.

Portsea, and the Great Ocean Road, and a lot of other places on Victoria's coast, are beautiful; but I admit to prejudice. If I was asked to show any visitor the one most typical and beautiful area of Australia, I would be touring them all over Sherbrooke Forest. It would help, I guess, if they were fit enough to take the tour with me by the most efficient and economical means still known to man — on foot.

Sherbrooke was the calm of my life for 15 years. This huge wooded area with its giant gums, ferny creeks and waterfalls is just on the outskirts of the city and, strangely enough for nowadays, its natural beauty has never been spoiled.

You'll never hear the cry "it's too crowded" — over eight hundred hectares of Forest Park would take 1,000 runners passing through it unnoticed.

I spent 16 years in competitive athletics, toured the world 20 to 30 times, and ran close to 1,000 races: yet my fondest memory of those years was the simple Sunday morning run in the Dandenongs to which I became addicted.

For me, everything came together during those early mornings in the forest with the sun filtering through the majestic gums, the air raw and crisp and the only sounds those of the birds chattering and squawking as we passed.

This was my routine for fifteen years — each Sunday morning in the Sherbrooke Forest Park. I first ran there in 1961 and I was still a regular six years after I finished international competitions in 1970.

Originally, only two or three of us would meet at a friend's house in Ferny Creek and then trek off through the forest paths, roving the hills, jumping the creeks through Sassafras, Olinda, Kallista, down to Belgrave, back up through the Upwey hills and into the Sherbrooke Forest for a drink at the falls and a jog back to the start. The variations were infinite. Sometimes, if we were racing later in the week, we would take a short loop of 10 or so miles; often, when I was preparing for an overseas tour, it would be out around the Silvan Dam and up the Board of Works track to the Olinda Golf Course (a 5 mile hill which gets steeper as it goes) — a trail of 23 or so miles.

The pioneering few have grown into regular groups of 50 or more as the complete perfection of the forest for long-distance training, and the sheer majesty of the place, became more widely known.

For those who do not have the time to make the 50-minute journey to Sherbrooke, there are Melbourne's renowned parks and gardens for strolling, walking or jogging. In the city itself, my very favourite place is the Royal Botanic Gardens. They are visited each day by thousands, yet their majestic beauty and serenity is always present.

The setting of Government House within the Gardens, plus the tan track (used daily by hundreds of athletes of all standards) adds to rather than detracts from their lustre. My friends and I had a regular path looping in and through the Gardens which we always ran when we wanted a break from the stress of our day-to-day training routine. The Gardens also boast the outdoor Myer Music Bowl which is an ideal setting for concerts. My fondest memory of the Bowl, though, is the annual Carols By Candlelight, organised on behalf of the Royal Victorian Institute for the Blind as one of Melbourne's memorable Christmas festivities.

I'm no bushman: I love city life — not in the smog-filled, smoky, traffic-choked cities most of the world's capitals have become, but a city like Melbourne. For me, Melbourne is close to my ideal of the proper setting for the perfect way of life.

The temperate climate means outdoor activities are possible summer and winter, and the city's parks and gardens are always in bloom.

Melbourne's size and layout guarantee enough alternative lifestyles to satisfy the whole spectrum of the human personality from financial magnate to beachcomber.

I'm convinced I'm living the good life in Victoria — people think because you're an athlete you must live some sort of Spartan life but it's not true. I keep my body fit so I can appreciate all the other things that are important to me. I like to eat at top grade restaurants, I like the theatre and beaches and tennis and Australian football, and getting to the office with the minimum of fuss.

In Melbourne you can do it all.

I can remember back to the 1956 Olympics when we had an enormous influx of people from overseas.

They loved our Australian pubs; and the Australian beer, light and cold, like lager, went down extremely well! To be honest, in 1956 that was about all we had to offer. I was only 19 at the time, so I was far from a man of the world, but since then both of us, City and boy, have grown up a lot.

Changes in the liquor licensing laws have had a lot to do with the change in Melbourne's nightlife. For too many years Victoria witnessed nightly the phenomenon of the "6 o'clock swill". People rushed away from work to gulp down as many drinks as possible — with, of course, nothing to eat — before the pubs closed at 6.00 p.m. Today Victoria's cities are more civilised and Melbourne's restaurants rate high on a world scale.

Glo Glo's and Two Faces in South Yarra have been high in my popularity lists for years, and still are, along with current favourites, The Willows and Fanny's. There are at least 50 others I like, representing every cuisine in the world. All the marvellous tastes of Europe are available, nearly all in restaurants run by natives of the country whose cooking they offer. Stir in the flavours of our Asian neighbours — Indonesian, Chinese, Japanese, and lately some lovely new Vietnamese places — and the atmosphere is practically complete.

I rate my favourite eating places not only on food, but also on atmosphere. I entertain a lot — besides being a runner I'm a businessman, and it's part of my job and my life to entertain people from out of town. I like to keep up with what's going on around the place — and there's an awful lot going on around Melbourne.

The look and feel of the City may be rapidly changing but the character and the essence of what Melbourne is all about is still there: alive but not brassy, energetic without being frantic. Simply put, it's a good place to live.

Drama on horseback — Lang Lang Rodeo.

Fun and games and civilization
Photography by Robert Gray.

Backing the winner — whether it runs on four legs or 36 — is a favourite Victorian sport.

◁
Flemington, home of the Melbourne Cup, is probably the best-known of Melbourne's four main race courses.

▷
Fighting it out at an Australian Rules football match are Richmond ("The Tigers", in yellow and black) and North Melbourne ("The 'Roos", in blue and white).

Kooyong — home of Australian tennis. Other popular sports include archery; rowing on the Yarra; jogging; golf (Victorian Peter Thomson) and cricket (Australia's Test Captain Kim Hughes faces the Englishmen at the M.C.G.)

Orienteering — growing in popularity; bird-watching at 'Coolart' on the Mornington Peninsula; and birds of a different feather, at Melbourne's Moomba Mardi Gras.

In the spirit of 'Life. Be in it' — the Melbourne Fun Run. (left)

On Melbourne's Port Phillip Bay — sailing, fishing, and just relaxing in the sun.

Carnival-time for young Victorians.

(Following page)
Some of Melbourne's 1300 restaurants —
offering everything from chips to chow mein,
soufflé to souvlaki.

Leisurely shopping at The Jam Factory,
Prahran; and the beachside market, St. Kilda.

Vintage cars in a bushland setting. For the cars, at least, it's all a bit of a yawn.

Haunt and habitat – and peace of mind

by Neil Douglas

Painter, conservationist and 'bush bunyip' Neil Douglas takes an unconventional look at the natural Victoria — Victoria beyond the cities.

". . . what it adds up to is that Australians are the world's most tamed people living among the world's strangest wild places."

Neil Douglas played a major role in setting up the Environmental Living Zone at Kangaroo Ground, about 40 minutes drive from Melbourne. Residents live "in the bush", in natural bushland alive with native animals and birds — but still within commuting distance of the city. The natural vegetation is protected by a policy of minimum land clearance, few fences, and no dogs, cats or other exotics.

The E.L.Z. was hailed as a planning precedent at the U.N. Conference on Human Settlements, Vancouver 1976.

This chapter's my shout — so have a beer!

Now that's a nice way for me to invite you into the Haunt and Habitat with me. "Haunt 'n' Habitat" is not the name of this pub I'm in, and don't anyone dare use it so. No, I'm sitting in the St. Andrew's, in the half-bush suburb of Eltham, 24 kilometres from the Melbourne G.P.O.

Eltham is best described as a 'habitat' where you will see many hairstyles — even on the Shire Council. And that's why there's some bush being saved. "Haunt 'n' habitat" puts a policeman, businessman and 'greenies' together on the local council, to keep the electors electric. In Eltham, the battle's on — over landscape and over the balance between tame and wild landscapes.

So while our representatives fight it out on the council, it's nice to sit having a quiet beer at the St. Andrew's. First let me tell you some funny stories before I give you the rundown on Victoria's haunts 'n' habitats. All about why the long-lost Leadbeater's Possum was lost, and about the extraordinary Fairy Penguins.

What to see is easy — Victoria is fun. But, for the traveller, how to feel about such a new environment is still an exciting question. The Bush can be difficult to appreciate because it has a kind of beauty that contradicts the European ideal. Eltham can be seen, perhaps, as something of a half-way house.

Sitting here, then, at the nice wooden tables on the wide, long verandah of this beaut country pub, I can see a couple of hundred relaxed-looking people at the Saturday morning market across the road — judges, greenies, managing directors, professors, policemen, drop-outs, M.P.'s, people in gardening gear, people at pie stalls; cabbages, leather hats, pot plants, geese, fruit, buskers. All this against the natural bush background of timbered hills, wild orchids and kangaroos, with a paddock or two snuggled in. Dinkum wild Victoria close to the city. Kids on horses, not an introduced tree in sight — Victoria at its best. With a climate noted as among the top for physical and mental stimulation (although we sometimes complain about the kind of stimulation it gives us).

A bush band often plays after dinner at the pub, and while you dance there's all the picture of what good living in Victoria is about. You feel grouse to be all together; kids with their families having a meal.

The landscape brings out the old bush ethic of mateship, makes for feeling peaceful together. The Red Gum Band plays: "Poor old Ned, you're better off dead — at least you've got peace of mind!" — from Edward Kelly, bushranger and Australian gentleman. (I've always wanted to speak real Australian, but I grew up with a New Zealand accent because Mum used to whip us if we pronounced anything incorrectly. It's hard to be one of the first painters trying to get down the true, wild Australia — and sound like a Pommy.)

Now let's get some more in, and tell some bush stories. Speaking real Okker, I think, on second thoughts, I wouldn't mind if they called this pub the Haunt and Habitat!

No scenic clichés, please!

An old Victorian bushman had been quietly listening to the tall tales his bush mates were spinning around the campfire. "Hey — come on, Bill!" they said finally. "You ain't said a word. It's your turn — right?"

Old Bill just puffed on his pipe. But at last he looked down very seriously at his boots and muttered, "Aw well, there was the time I drove a mob of 44-gallon drums from Victoria to Tasmania." A pause — and an expectant silence. Finally someone said, "Well — how on earth did you get across Bass Strait?" Old Bill took another puff, looked at him and growled, "Aw — I didn't go that way."

Well, I'm not going to drive a mob of my best 44-gallon words into a list of Victoria's scenic clichés. All tourists have heard it before — "See this, it is unique!" And even, "Don't miss that, it's even more unique!" So I want to be like Old Bill the drum-duffer and go a different way; and start by saying that how Victorians relate to the wild means we must first have a look at the Wild Victorian!

To call Victoria "Down Under" sounds as topsy-turvy to us — sitting upright here in the St. Andrew's — as the idea of all those English and European and American people with their heads hanging down and their feet pointing up towards ours. Why doesn't their beer fall out?

So Victorians can dare to be different. What a wonderful opportunity — different ideas, different animals, different plants, different landscapes, new experiences and new feelings in a different world. Surely all these make an opportunity to express ourselves in a different way — a way that should be fascinating for world travellers.

For example, what other community could tell the whole world that the Yarra River, where you can still find the prehistoric platypus in the city area, was the only river in the world where the bottom runs on the top? Victoria is full of laughter, especially if Edna Everage or Phillip Adams are around.

Yet, difference for no reason is pointless. So how can we find any inspiration in these Victorian differences? Can we break away from overseas ideas and fashions and present both ourselves and our intelligent visitors with something memorable and worthwhile? I hear a sceptical voice mutter: You mean like Myer Doncaster, the new department store they built in the cow paddocks? Like Canberra, Australia's hygienic capital? Well, is it so difficult being different? Do we want to show our tourists what they're trying to get away from? Like black angus cattle in the bright green paddock? Of course, we've got golf courses and swimming pools and wonderful things to play with, right, but out there is the unique, the wild Victoria.

I read once that there were four hundred landscape architects attached to American Forestry. I thought: "We haven't got any — and it's a ripper idea." So I went to see the top Forests man in Victoria and (after the public service people agreed) he got three. He also let me address the Forestry school at Creswick about the tame and wild approach to landscape, and defining a balance. My friend Abbie said I was

wasting my time: they couldn't see trees for wood, and they would all have short back and sides. But none of them did, and that day went really well.

After a beaut talk under the fine old introduced trees of Creswick, with the half dozen paintings of sheer unusable bushscrub I took up with me, I left with a feeling that when these people graduated and began working for Victoria, we needn't have fears about keeping tame and wild landscapes in balance.

Remember — Victoria is the Garden State. What sort of garden? Pine tree gardens, farming gardens, and wild gardens!

What people see of Victoria's haunt 'n' habitat will be conditioned by how adventurous their outlook is. So let's have a look at a young Victorian in the making — my daughter Biddy — then at the wild adults who both represent Victoria and show it off to the world.

Victoria was 98% British when I was boy and in those days every child of 5 knew about "Home" and what London meant. To test this, I called Biddy once when she was 5 and asked a trick question — What is the capital of London? She didn't know. What's the capital of New York, then? Still she didn't know. Well, I asked, beginning to get desperate, what's the capital of Melbourne? Without a second's hesitation the answer came — "Eltham", she said. At first I just giggled: and then I was delighted. "Right!" I replied, laughing, "Good on you, Biddy — how right you are!"

Now don't you laugh. It's a bright, shining, new, clean thing to begin life in a new world, innocent of all the old hangovers and hangups. Lost, if you like — alright, lost — away down here in the wilds of the Southern Ocean along with the Fairy Penguins and Leadbeater's Possum, and

"The long wash of Australasian seas".

At last, the obeisance, the allegiance, the cultural cringe is over! To Biddy's generation, Home is here! Her generation will not be calling motels and guesthouses Chateau Fountainbleau and Dorset Close, and covering the land with Oaks and Elms. A little story, but a big thing.

The Old World can seem very pompous indeed to a growing child in this new world. This is where convict William Buckley, who escaped in 1803, wandered for 32 years with the wild Aborigines along the untouched shores of Melbourne so recently, and forgot the whole English language except for the word "butter". Butter, indeed — butter in the trackless bush. And still there today is the same butterless primal Banksia scrub he wandered in, full of strange honey-smelling but moonstruck wild flowers. Still today so many beaches in Victoria have nothing on them but kangaroo tracks where the roos have raced away down the sheening beaches in the empty dawns.

And now I suppose it's my solemn duty to investigate the adult Victorian to see how he or she represents Victoria.

The Wild and the tame

• The truism has it: "Australia is the most urban community in the world." Victorians are certainly very much a part of that scene.

• Darwin said you could divide the world into Australia and the rest of the world and of the two, the Australian haunt and habitat was the more strange and interesting.

So, what it adds up to is that Australians are the world's most tamed people living among the world's strangest wild places.

Don't shoot through though: categorically, this fact provides residents and visitors with a golden opportunity. Everywhere you go in Victoria, you can have all the benefits of high living standards, right next door to the world's most ancient landscapes. Here the marsupials and monotremes from the Lizard Age still walk around in broad daylight, and lots of plants and animals are living fossils.

So watch out that your holiday guides and brochures don't waste your time showing you the sort of thing you might have paid all those dollars to fly away from. I read in *The Age* that tourists are spending more than half a billion dollars a year in Victoria — so get your money's worth and do here what you'll never be able to do in London and Las Vegas and all those other organized places.

If you want to see the wild as well as the tame, Victoria is the ideal place. Unlike Africa or the Amazon, it's quite easy — easier, maybe, than anywhere else in the world — to encounter the world's strangest wild. Everything from desert to snow — including the world's tallest hardwoods.

Try venturing fearlessly into the Victorian wilderness for at least one metre from the safety of the friendly road. Keeping your eye out for direction, recite after me —
"There's a river in the Range
I love to think about.
Perhaps the searching feet of change
Have never found it out."

Remember, this whole land has enjoyed the world's longest holiday. See how the roadless, trackless forest comes down from the Ranges to the river, then up the other side again to the tops.

So many places in Victoria where the foot of white man still has never trodden are within your reach. Some of them are only minutes from your motel. No gorillas, no old castles, no naughty golden sculptures — but parrots, Crimson Rosellas and dusty-pink Galahs seen fleetingly in the haunted blue bush. There is peace of mind here, as maybe nowhere else on earth. Just you and evolution . . . and your nice restaurant dinner in the evening, as usual.

Don't take a pretty girl into the bush

I was trying to explain to a beautiful girl why I painted our wild and woolly bush. I was having an exhibition at Melbourne's Toorak Gallery, and there was this influential, cultured and well educated girl.

Tall she was, and well-read. Asked me why no Australian artists painted water like Turner's, with lots of dots of light. I started to say our water wasn't like that — not only in appearance, but in what it *meant* in this driest of continents, when a voice broke in — one of the strangers at the exhibition, and an unwelcome interruption to our tête-a-tête.

"How do they come?" he said, waving his arm at the painting.

"Oh, the usual way", I said, rather unwillingly. "I just paint on the spot, and then in the studio, until they look like what I am feeling."

"Aw, I don't getcha — I mean, do they come *framed* or not?" He was wearing pants with a red stripe down his leg. His way of speaking was genuine Okker. The girl looked incredulous.

"Yes, of course", I said.

"Well — I'll take that one", he said quietly, pointing to my favourite (and most expensive) big one — of very wild and scraggy bush. Difficult to appreciate — especially for a bloke in striped trousers. I guess I shared the girl's incredulity.

"Why do you like it?" I said slowly, suddenly feeling a bit awkward.

"Well, I'm a tram driver", the stranger said. "I drive the tram down Toorak Road out there, and I see this big photer of yours in the Gallery winder. And I nearly fell out the tram. Next time I'm coming down I stop the tram for no reason for a moment and have another gawp, while the conductor's banging on the bell."

He went on . . . "Today's my day off, see? And I've come in to buy it. I'm a pack-horse man, see? The reason is, my wife's died, the kids are married, and I'm still young enough. So I take a pack horse and get away from all the bells in me ears. I know all the wild deserts and the Snowy Ranges like the back of me hand — swamps, beaches, caves, heaths, deserts and mountains — the lot. And then when I see this real big photo of pack-horse country, I love it. Even the paint looks wild."

"Well, at least you know what I'm trying to paint", I said, looking around for the girl. She had gone. Taking her carefully cultivated culture with her, insulated safely away from anything to do with the local sources of our culture — Victoria's land and life. Victoria in the real. Perhaps true culture always springs from the uncultured. Standing there with the bell-sick tram driver in the Gallery, I knew that he, a tram driver, really felt that thing in the sticks — the thing that D. H. Lawrence, a coalminer's son, meant when he wrote that "Australia has never been loved". So many paintings of Australia in modern styles inspired from — overseas. And the trammie loved the bush not as a 'Resource', or somewhere tidily labelled "natural environment", but for itself, as it was for 200 million years before it became a management exercise. David Herbert would have liked my tram driver. He really felt for Victoria, with love. You can say that again, with bells on!

Are gumleaves green?

Melbourne writer Alan Marshall, who has a world voice, can help us now. He talked to me one day when he was living in a caravan near our home in the bush.

"You artists are terrible people", he grinned. "When I first looked at the bush I used to see Streetons and Hysens; later on, after seeing their work I could see Pughs and Nolans and Percevals and Boyds in the bush. Now you've ruined my eyes again — everywhere I see a damned Neil Douglas. But this thing you're painting now is terrible — it's too green. The bush is blue, grey, brown — not that vivid green like a fire. Have you been on the gum juice?" He wouldn't believe me when I said that gum leaves could be like green fire, with the light through them.

But in a little while, he called me over to his caravan. "Sit there — no, on that side of the table where I write. Now look up, look through the window". Outside was a curtain of extremely green gum leaves, with the light through them — just like the painting I was doing.

"I've sat in that seat for two years," he said, "writing: 'This is the grass' and 'In my own heart', and I've never noticed how green those leaves were until I saw it in the painting and didn't believe it. You're right — they can be greener than deciduous trees."

If you really want to appreciate our Miss Victoria, have a look at what the artists and writers and film-makers have made of her. This can really enrich your own idea of her beauty. In the old paintings — like those of Buvelot — they used to think it proper to paint our gum trees as if they were Oaks. Later, they painted as if gum trees were 'The

Monarch of the Glen'. But today for the first time our writers and artists and filmmakers are coming to grips with something totally new in this primeval land. Something which is novel and difficult for Europeans and other travellers and even Australians, to appreciate: style originating *here*.

Blue Poles in Victoria

'Blue Poles' was being hung in the National Gallery of Victoria, and the local T.V. station rang me. Would I do an interview for the news on the controversial painting? "I warn you — I like Jackson Pollock," I told them. "That's alright — we just want your comments", they said — although I felt it was a trap for a landscape painter.

From memory, the interview went something like this.

"Well, Neil Douglas, why do you like 'Blue Poles'?"

"It's what Victoria looked like to the pioneers," I said. "And it's about today's encounter with the wilds of space. It's about the chaos in order, and the order in chaos. Modern man must understand wildness to survive. If he thinks he can tame everything, he'll end up with the shrinks."

"Is it worth a million dollars?"

"Anything that can help Australians love the wildness of the bush is worth a million dollars."

I am quite serious in saying that there's something in common with the bush in the wild, ordered disarray of 'Blue Poles'.

The early European settlers and travellers called this land drab, monotonous, drought-stricken — anything but green. The explorer Dampier called Australia: "This most miserable of all countries." Today we know that there is beauty in the desert.

An old lady who flew into Melbourne's Tullamarine Airport at the age of 90 interested the reporters at the airport when they found out she had come, unaccompanied, on her first visit to Australia — and she was meeting no-one. She explained that she had been the wife of a sea-captain. Her first voyage had been her honeymoon at the age of 18.

The couple lived on a trading vessel, plying around the Cape of Good Hope and Cape Horn, and back again.

On her first trip she noticed afar off a great blaze of light in the sky — a silvery, shining reflection. She asked her husband the captain what was the light in the sky.

He replied, "That's Australia — that's where Australia is".

Talking to the reporters, the old lady said, "No other continent has it. It was always there as we sailed past. I have always wanted to come and see what manner of life, what plants and flowers and animals, live under that great blaze of light in the sky."

Very often in overseas exhibitions, art critics have noted the brilliant quality of the light in Australian paintings. There seems to be an inspiration in the land itself, in the primal atmosphere, which has nothing to do with European or Asian inspiration.

Wild Fire

Earth, air, fire, water: the four primeval elements of landscape and life. In this driest of continents, earth and air — the fundamentals of habitat — are affected by fire more than anywhere else on earth.

Victoria is the most fire-prone landscape in the world. An introduction to it would be misleading without mention of the dramatic, even traumatic, part played by fire in the life of its people, its flora and fauna, and the reflection in art of all these living things.

Images of Victoria are reflected in heat as much as light. For here, far from being the terrible demon it is called, wild fire brings an amazing beauty and an amazing resilience in the behaviour of its plants and animals and in human relations.

I guess I'm out of time. You'll have to see the touring people about where to go for the famous Fairy Penguins and the long-lost Leadbeater's Possum. Sorry about that. But the main thing is — see Victoria both ways: the tame and the primal. A beer for the road. See you later!

Haunt and habitat . . . and peace of mind
Photography by Paul Olson.

"Earth, air, fire, water: the four primeval elements of landscape and life."

The Australian environment is one of extremes.

Prolonged drought may be followed by weeks of flooding: wildfires can destroy whole forests overnight. Man works to bring these swings "under control": but for the plants and animals which have always been here, the rule is, "adapt or perish".

Marsupials, like this wombat, obtain moisture from the vegetation they eat — and so are unworried when the creeks dry up in summer.

Mountain Ash forests, like the one opposite, are naturally regenerated by bushfires, which not only destroy the trees but clear away the undergrowth — allowing the new seedlings a year's head-start from the understorey which otherwise would shade them out. Mountain Ash is Leadbeater's Possum country: it also covers the catchment for Melbourne's fine water supply.

(Following page):
The Grampians, where the eucalypts along the crests are adapted to poor soil and baking summers. In the valleys there are Red Gums, which make the most of wet feet in winter.

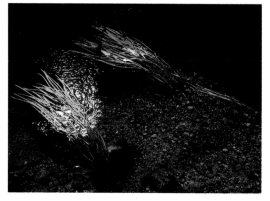

"Modern man must understand wildness to survive."

The Great Dividing Range extends in Victoria from near Mt. Kosciusko (New South Wales) south and west, finishing spectacularly in the Grampians. Mountain Ash occurs in the middle altitudes, with Alpine Ash above it and Messmate/Peppermint in the foothills. Echidnas ("Australian ant-eaters") are found in drier mountain areas.

On the forest floor, only those species which can flourish in low light conditions, with wet soils in winter and dry conditions in summer, can survive.

"... the chaos in order and the order in chaos."

Here and there, in the high rainfall areas, are pockets of lush temperate rain forest and tree ferns. Creeks and cascading waterfalls add to the pervading sense of wetness: vegetation includes ancient forms like the spiky Blackboy and the Banksia, beloved by honey-eaters. The best of these areas are now protected in National Parks, including Glenaladale, Alfred and Lind National Parks.

More restrained, but just as ancient, are the Antarctic Beech forests, which grow in association with Mountain Ash. Beech trees have a delicately patterned "fiddleback" woodgrain, and around the turn of the century they were extensively cut down to make fine furniture and musical instruments. As a result, these magnificent forests have now almost disappeared in Victoria: remnants can be seen in the Otway Ranges and around Cambarville.

"Today we know there is beauty in the desert."

The north-west of Victoria is hot and dry: the land of the Big Desert, the Little Desert and the Sunset Country. Flocks of brilliantly-coloured parrots — and, in springtime, the wildflowers — provide relief from a muted palette of yellows, browns and endless blues. Mallee eucalypts (the explorers' nightmare — too small to climb, too big to see over) spread across the featureless landscape, providing shelter for the mound-building Lowan or Mallee Fowl, kangaroos, and a great variety of reptiles. Here and there, gypsum saltpans — remnants of a prehistoric ocean — reduce the vegetation to salt-tolerant succulents, or maybe nothing at all.

Much of this country has been cleared for wheat and sheep farming, but typical mallee scrub can still be seen in such National Parks as Hattah-Kulkyne, Wyperfeld and the Little Desert; the Big Desert Wilderness; and the Wathe Faunal Reserve.

"There is a peace of mind here, as maybe nowhere else on earth. Just you and evolution . . ."

The 90-mile beach forms the sand-barrier between the Gippsland Lakes and Bass Strait, and the fragile primary dune is constantly changing: moulded by the winds and waves of the storms of Bass Strait. You can often walk for miles here, without seeing anyone else.

Offshore reefs and their associated rocky headlands — like these at Cape Liptrap — support a rich variety of marine plants and animals, and have been the subject of

considerable biological research. Less happily, they have featured in a good many of the shipwrecks that dot the Victorian coast.

'**What people see of Victoria's haunt 'n habitat will be conditioned by how adventurous their outlook is.**'

It's easy to miss much of the interest in the Victorian landscape — particularly in the more developed areas. Animals are shy and often nocturnal; flowers can sometimes be small and hidden. But for those with eyes to see, there is a constant drama in the Australian bush.

Some things, of course, are quite easy to see like flocks of Sulphur-crested Cockatoos and Corellas which feed on farming areas, much to the annoyance of the wheat farmers; or the Pink Heath, Victoria's floral emblem, which is quite common both in the bush and in suburban gardens.

Dotted throughout the farming areas are rocky outcrops and remnants of native vegetation, adding some landscape interest and providing important havens for wildlife in an altered landscape.

78

All art is at once surface and symbol.
Those who go beneath the surface do so
at their peril.
— Oscar Wilde

If you ask me what I came to do in this
world, I, an artist, I will answer you: "I
am here to live out loud."
— Emile Zola

Without tradition, art is a flock of sheep
without a shepherd. Without innovation,
it is a corpse.
— Winston Churchill

You use a glass mirror to see your face:
you use works of art to see your soul.
— George Bernard Shaw

Victoria—
State of the Arts

by Phillip Adams

Art is what you make it . . . whether
it be a heady concoction of illusion and
reality as in a scene from "Momma's Little
Horror Show", or an amusing reflection
on the facts by satirist Phillip Adams —
who, in this essay, like Momma's face
behind the action (opposite), seems to
have his tongue firmly in his cheek.

Complementing the text, photographs
by Rennie Ellis present a true-to-life
reflection of the Arts in Victoria.

With those quotations from Victorians
prominent in the arts, I hope to dignify
my small contribution to this volume. I
have approached my task (a brief
overview of Victoria's massive and
breathtaking contribution to the arts) with
the appropriate earnestness, devoting
many minutes to in-depth research.

Consequently, I'm able to report that
Victoria is home to a prodigious number
of people who, amongst other things, pot,
pen, pluck, paint, puppet, pas de deux,
poetise, perform, parade, publish,
patronise, plagiarise, portray, produce,
pose and play the piano, oft with passion
and panache. Plus, there's a peck of
pitiful pundits who've a perverse
penchant for prolonged alliteration.

Prominent visitors who expected to
find Victoria a haven for bouncing
marsupials and neanderthal footballers
may be surprised by my resumé of down-
under Renaissance, a veritable
quattrocento of culture. However the
photographs that embellish my words will
provide the necessary proof.

As visitors are quick to realise,
Melbourne is Venice with asphalt canals,
Florence on the Yarra. Sophisticated
jetsetters concur that the part of the city
known as "the Paris end of Collins Street"
is every bit as chic as that section of Paris
known as the Melbourne end of the
Champs Elyssées. And while other nations
may boast about their city's squares
(Leicester, Red, Times, Trafalgar, etc.)

all concede the superiority of Melbourne's, one that concentrates *all* the most popular ingredients into an area one-tenth the size.

What is Michelangelo's St. Peter's beside East Melbourne's St. Patrick's? What is Mardi Gras compared to Melbourne's Moomba? What has the Forbidden City beside our Little Bourke Street? Can there be any doubt that Victoria is the true seat of civilisation, and that such off-Broadway civilisations as the Roman and the Greek are mere arrivistes?

Perceptive visitors will note that our Shrine of Remembrance, built overlooking the Yarra, contains a number of eerily familiar architectural elements. Built by the Anzacs, the first Australians, the Shrine has inspired the great pyramids of Egypt and Mexico whilst the soaring columns of the portico provided the inspiration for the Parthenon and, hence, the Roman Forum. While the origins of the Shrine are shrouded in mystery, it is clear it was Victoria and *not* Von Danniken's astronauts that seeded a score of ancient cultures.

Even in modern times, Victoria has been a global inspiration, the mecca for every muse. Take the French Impressionists. It is clear that they established themselves through skilful industrial espionage, by *anticipating* our fabled Heidelberg School of Painters. And it's a matter of cold, hard fact that Melbourne made the world's first feature films — and that kinematic kidnapping led to the establishment of Hollywood.

It's amazing how very few people who are famous in *any* branch of the arts are not Victorians or Melburnians. While it's true that Leo Tolstoy was a Russian and that Herman Melville worked for the Customs service in the U.S., they're the rule-proving exceptions. Virtually everyone else who's made a major contribution to culture, from Dame Nellie Melba to Dame Edna Everage, were Melbourne-born.

There's Fred Williams painting his beaut landscapes out near the Toorak Drive-In; with Neil Douglas and Clifton Pugh paddling their palettes in the nearby bush. There's an artistic ziggurat

shaped like Kaiser Bill's helmet going up next to the river, and a brand new Performing Arts Centre shaped like the Fuehrerbunker in Geelong. We've got five regional arts centres and sixteen regional art galleries, including one at Benalla run by Len French's daughter, where Tom Roberts from Heidelberg meets paintings by Emmanuel Phillips Fox.

Visitors to Melbourne cannot but be charmed by the number plates on our vehicles, proclaiming Victoria The Garden State. It may be of interest to know that these marvellous pieces of folk art are lovingly fashioned by Her Majesty's prisoners at Pentridge Jail. In what other country are the criminal classes so dedicated to beauty?

I understand that in New York the subway trains are painted by vandals brandishing aerosols. In Melbourne, to discourage such amateur self-expression, our trams have been painted by famed artists. If you visit us long enough, you may have the opportunity to travel on a Mirka Mora tram or a Clifton Pugh tram. So while San Francisco can boast its cable cars, Melbourne has invented the mobile mural, the electric fresco. To fully grasp the originality of the notion, imagine waiting at a bus stop in Rome to take a ride on the Sistine Ceiling.

Melbourne is also a city of thespian tendencies. Hence the extraordinary number of its theatres, far more than you'd expect from a metropolis of its size. Here the works of David Williamson and Jack Hibberd are performed, along with those of comparatively obscure dramatists, like Shakespeare, Tennessee Williams and Harold Pinter.

Despite its vast antiquity, Melbourne is mercifully free of the ugly ruins that so deface European cities, attracting such undesirable elements as guides, cats and tourists. In Melbourne nothing is allowed to get more than 50 years old before being ripped down and replaced. Admittedly, our developers have been slackening in their efforts of late and a number of older buildings, including New Orleans-style wrought iron terraces, gracious colonial mansions and other anachronisms may still be observed.

We wish to apologise to distinguished visitors for such lapses while reassuring them that, with a little bit of luck and hard work, we should be able to get rid of the remaining relics by the turn of the century.

A regrettable lapse, for instance, has been to take the old North Melbourne Meat Market, vaulted ceilings and all, and turn it into the best craft centre in the country. We should be able to get rid of the potters, the weavers and the candlestickmakers in short order and replace them once more with trotters, chops and lights.

Yet may I admit to just a hint of sentiment? A little nostalgia for some of the buildings of yesteryear? For example, I remember with affection, the underground loos that were the Louvres of Melbourne, owing to the erotic murals (executed with all the primitive power of the cave painters of Lascaux) which could be studied at one's leisure. And while Athens had the Acropolis, Melbourne had the State Theatre, a cinema that contained not only an upsurging wurlitzer, but the most dazzling array of nude statuary all mixed up with Moorish balustrades.

Mind you, we still have Luna Park at St. Kilda Beach, a structure as remarkable in its architecture as any of mad King Ludwig's castles, where visitors walk through a gaping mouth into a whirl of centrifugal fantasies. After a few minutes at Luna Park, with its Big Dipper, Ghost Train and River Caves, a visit to Disneyland would seem sadly anti-climatic.

Yet we Victorians are in no way provincials. We're not suggesting that cities like Paris and Prague, Amsterdam and Athens, Manhattan and Madrid are completely Philistine. It's just that they don't measure up to the stature or statues of Melbourne. While the Louvre has Rodin thinking, we have, in Flinders Street, a giant bronze of Matthew Flinders *discovering*. He stands proudly at the prow of a boat, the rest of which is missing. (It's just as well the sculptor never got round to doing the remainder of the vessel as its stern would be thrusting into St. Paul's Cathedral.)

We also have Sir Thomas Blamey, a war time hero, standing up grasping the windscreen of an otherwise non-existent jeep. As with Michelangelo's half-chiselled giants in Florence, these unfinished works convey a feeling of energy and vitality.

For generations the world's most famous painting was on display in Melbourne, in Young and Jackson's pub. A full length nude of a young lady known as Chloe, it was infinitely superior to that heavily shrouded Mona Lisa. Melbourne is also the home of the world's greatest theatrical performer in Dame Edna Everage, a remarkable woman who, in the tradition of Radclyffe Hall, sometimes dons male garb and writes under the pseudonym of Barry Humphries.

However, our artistic scene is not free of problems. Recently there has been a most alarming outbreak of macramé, undoubtedly the most repugnant art form ever devised. This sort of abstract knitting, this pretentious form of knot-tying, is causing great concern to true aesthetes like myself. Scientists at the CSIRO are working overtime in the hope of developing something to get the macramé plague under control.

The wonderful thing about Melbourne is that it offers such cultural diversity. Not only have a high proportion of Victorians abandoned such countries as Italy, Greece, France, England, Ireland, Yugoslavia, the USSR and New Zealand to live in this, the nexus of everything worthwhile in human culture, but they've brought with them sufficient of their own arts and craft to make extensive, expensive tourism quite unnecessary. You can eat just about anything in Melbourne, from frogs' legs to falafel, while a Little Bourke Street dim sim makes a visit to mainland China quite redundant.

It's the same with our Art Gallery; if you go to Italy and trudge through the Uffizi, all you'll see are endless rooms full of Renaissance paintings — Madonnas with child and Saint Sebastians porcupined with arrows. If you go to Amsterdam, the Rijks Museum is simply stuffed with Rembrandts and there are halls full of Hals. And I well remember that on visiting the Tate in London, I was tyrannised by Turners.

Our National Gallery of Victoria houses Australia's best art collection, containing one or two of just about every school of art, thus saving your travellers' cheques and varicose veins. Now there's no need to go trudging all over Europe where you're likely to be mugged, begged at or bored.

There's no point going to Sydney, either. While they have difficulty staging full-scale opera in the Opera House, the Victorian Arts Centre beneath the tower/spire/spike will have room for simultaneous performances of *Aida* in the State House, *Lear* in the Playhouse, something avant-garde in the Studio, and still have room for troops of other troupes in the foyer, on the stairs, under the waterfall and up on the antenna.

Finally, while visiting Victoria I urge you to take in a couple of new-wave Australian films, such as my most recent effort, "Claws", an adventure-film about a killer yabbie.* Not to mention my moving adaption of D. H. Lawrence's little known novel "Wombat".

*Small Australian freshwater lobster.

Victoria's new Arts Centre, under construction near the Yarra River. The National Gallery of Victoria can be seen behind the Arts Centre.

Victoria — State of the Arts
Photography by Rennie Ellis.

The Australian Opera seen here presenting "The Tales of Hoffmann" at the Palais Theatre, Melbourne, is Australia's national opera company, specialising in Grand Opera. Like the Victoria State Opera, which often commissions contemporary works, the Australian Opera is frequently on tour. Australia has producd some of the world's finest singers, including Joan Sutherland, Joan Hammond, Donald Smith and Robert Dowd.

▷

The Australian Ballet is based in Melbourne.
The Ballet tours widely in Australia and
overseas, performing established classics and
modern works including those commissioned
especially for the company. Students at the
Australian Ballet School are selected from the
best young talent throughout Australia.

▷ (lower right)

Since 1976 the Victorian and South Australian
Governments have jointly funded the
Australian Dance Theatre, one of Australia's
most exciting and innovative modern dance
companies. In 1980 the Australian Dance
Theatre represented Australia at the
Edinburgh Festival and toured Europe and
Asia. Artistic Director, Jonathon Taylor, chats
here with dancers prior to a workshop
performance for Melbourne school children.

▽

The One Extra Dance Theatre is an
experimental ensemble formed in 1976 with
the aim of expanding the parameters of dance
as theatre.

The Melbourne Symphony Orchestra performing at the Melbourne Town Hall under the baton of its Chief Conductor, Hiroyuki Iwaki. The Melbourne Symphony Orchestra is one of Australia's finest orchestras and boasts a large and loyal home-town audience. It is jointly funded by the Australian Broadcasting Commission, the Victorian Government, the City of Melbourne and the University of Melbourne.

◁
Melbourne is a recognised performance venue for major international artists. Here celebrated Yugoslavian cellist Valter Despalj gives a recital at the Dallas Brooks Hall.

The stained glass ceiling by Melbourne artist Leonard French is a stunning feature of the Great Hall of the National Gallery of Victoria. The Great Hall is a popular venue for concerts: this is one of the free Sunday afternoon C.B.A. Bank Prom Concerts.

Full time students at the Victorian College of the Arts — which offers courses in music, drama and dance and nurtures many fine talents — have the opportunity to perform their own works in public before graduation.

▷
Trad jazz is alive and well and living in Melbourne. The Jazz Experience is one of many jazz combos playing at hotels and restaurants around the city.

◁
With its multi-national culture, Victoria enjoys a variety of ethnic talent. Greek Tassos Ioannidis and his brother Christos are composer/performers who directed the experimental music programme at the La Mama Theatre for 5 years. They have performed with the Melbourne Symphony Orchestra, but also take their music into factories and schools.

◁ (far left)
Two composers with different styles: Brian Brown (pictured at The Commune, an avant garde jazz venue) is one of Australia's outstanding jazz composers and reed players; George Dreyfus is renowned for his T.V. drama themes as well as his innovative opera, orchestral and choral works.

Some of Melbourne's young people get their first taste of performing in public by "busking" in the city streets — adding colourful entertainment, and often real talent, to the Melbourne scene. Some could end up as successful as Melbourne-born Margaret Roadnight, one of Australia's most exciting and best-known blues and folk performers.

▷
The highly individual New Zealand rock band Split Enz has seen its albums reach the top of the Australian charts. The band, which is building up an overseas reputation, got its first breaks on the Melbourne pub music circuit.

▽
Ross Wilson is one of Victoria's best-known, home-grown rock and roll writer/performers. An original member of Daddy Cool, one of the first Australian rock bands to perform in the U.S., Ross currently leads Mondo Rock. He is also highly regarded as a record producer and nurturer of young talent.

Melbourne-born Renee Gayer is amongst the best and most versatile female performers on the Australian rock scene. She has recorded albums both in Australia and the United States and is renowned for her powerful, black-blues style voice and her rivetting stage performances.

International stars regularly visit Melbourne, which is recognised for its big, enthusiastic concert audiences. Here Bob Dylan — composer singer, poet and born-again Christian — performs at the Myer Music Bowl, a huge outdoor venue located in the Domain gardens adjacent to the city.

Many of Australia's leading contemporary artists live in Victoria. Here are some of them.

◁ (far left)
Asher Bilu: Born in Tel Aviv, he arrived in Victoria in 1957. His large scale abstract paintings use built-up surface textures and tensions and often employ complex three dimensional planes to convey visions of cosmic forces. He has won the Blake Prize for religious art.

◁
Donald Friend: After periods in Australia, Europe and Africa painter and writer Donald Friend lived for many years in Bali before returning to Melbourne in 1980. His strongly romantic, figurative paintings have been acquired by major Australian galleries and collected internationally.

▷
Clifton Pugh: One of Australia's best-known painters. Noted for his striking portraits (which have won him three Archibald Prizes) and his evocation of the Australian bush and its creatures. This exhibition at Realities Gallery was a result of a six week camp in Arnhem Land in the Northern Territory with Sydney painter Frank Hodgkinson (seated left).

◁ (far left)
Peter Corlett: A Melbourne sculptor who specialises in lifesize figurative works done in fibreglass. In 1981 he returned from the U.K. where he successfully worked and spent a year as Artist-in-Residence at Exeter University.

◁
Fred Williams: Acclaimed as Australia's leading landscape painter, Williams enjoys an international reputation for his paintings which transform the monotony of the bush into a source of beauty and rare spiritual power. He is the only Australian painter to have a one-man show at New York's prestigious Museum of Modern Art.

▷
Murray Walker: Ballarat born and now living in Melbourne, his lyrical paintings and etchings have been exhibited widely in Australia. He is also recognised for his book "Pioneer Crafts of Early Australia".

◁

The sculpture courtyard at the National Gallery of Victoria — in the foreground, "Seated Figure" by Henry Moore. The National Gallery is Australia's oldest public gallery and houses the nation's finest art collection. There are also 16 regional public art galleries serving the rest of Victoria.

This ceramic animal sculpture fountain by Elaine Katzer is especially popular with the thousands of young visitors to the Melbourne Zoo. It is one of many unusual fountains seen around the city and its surrounding gardens.

The Victorian Tapestry Workshop, established by the State Government in 1976, is the only one of its kind in Australia and receives commissions from around the world. The wattle tapestry on the left is now hanging in Melbourne's new Wentworth Hotel; the Aboriginal motif tapestry, designed by Charlie Taruru, is destined for the new Victorian Arts Centre.

Dinosaurs march along the fence of the National Museum of Victoria, with a little help from their friends. The National Museum is noted, among other things, for its extensive collection of Aboriginal and Polynesian Art.

This tram, painted by artist and dollmaker Mirka Mora, is one of several decorated by Victorian artists under the sponsorship of the Ministry for the Arts.

The Herald Outdoor Art Show is a regular feature of Melbourne's Moomba festival, and offers public exposure for many amateur painters.

▷

A number of prominent banks and companies in Victoria have made major art purchases for the walls of their private and public chambers. These tapestries by John Coburn are on permanent public display at the A.N.Z. Bank headquarters.

The Royal Melbourne Institute of Technology was originally founded in 1887 as the The Working Men's College. This mural by Geoff Hogg depicts changes in the R.M.I.T. environment over the last century.

Animator, graphic designer and writer Alex Stitt is responsible for many memorable illustrated messages, including Norm and the "Life. Be In It" campaign. He also created the animated feature film, "Grendel, Grendel, Grendel".

◁
As well as exhibiting the works of major Australian artists, Georges Mora and his son William of the Tolarno Galleries in South Yarra have brought important shows by European masters to Melbourne. There are many commercial galleries in Melbourne and regional cities, offering a constantly changing programme of exhibitions.

Melbourne sculptor Matcham Skipper and his son Adam at work on a wooden mural for the Rural Finance Commission. Skipper, also highly regarded as a silversmith and jewellery designer, lives and works at the "Monsalvat" artists colony which was established at Eltham in the 1930's by Justus Jorgensen.

Art on the grand scale — a monumental mosaic under preparation at the State Studio in Melbourne. Designed by artist Harold Freedman, the 25 metre high mural symbolises the Greek legend of fire and is destined for the Eastern Hill Station of the Metropolitan Fire Brigade.

▷ (upper right)
Jack Hibberd, Australian playwright, is best known for his one-man play "A Stretch of the Imagination", the hilarious "Dimboola", and "A Toast to Melba".

Author Helen Garner, whose first novel "Monkey Grip' won the 1978 National Book Council Book of the Year Award. It was recently made into a film. Her latest book is "Honour and other people's children".

▷
Melbourne film-makers Don McLennan (Director) and Peter Friedrich (Director of photography and Editor), whose movie "Hard Knocks" won the Jury Prize and Best Actress Award in the 1980 Australian Film Institute Awards.

Film director Tim Burstall directs a scene in a train carriage, during the filming of "Partners", a contemporary drama by acclaimed Melbourne author David Williamson.

◁ (left to right)
Joy Dunstan and Neild Schneider in a scene from Harold Pinter's play "Landscape" presented at La Mama theatre, a tiny coffee-house theatre in Carlton.

Irene Inescort and Keith Michell in the Melbourne Theatre Company production of Michell's play "Pete McGynty and The Dreamtime". The Melbourne Theatre Company is Australia's largest professional theatre company.

Malcolm Robertson rehearses Gerda Nicolson, Caroline Gillmer and Peter Cummins for the Playbox Theatre Company's production of "I Sent a Letter to My Love".

◁ (left to right)
At the Moving Artz Dance Studio in Fitzroy, John Thompson, Rinske Ginsberg and Lynden Nicholls — collectively known as "3's a Company" — rehearse a performance piece.

Circus Oz, a unique Australian phenomenon which combines traditional circus stunts with a zany range of unusual theatrical talents, toured Europe in 1980 to thunderous applause.

Students at the Melbourne State College design and make costumes for a college production of "The Birds" by Aristophanes.

◁ (left to right)
Graeme Blundell was a foundation member of the Australian Performing Group, a co-op of actors, directors and writers which introduced Melbourne audiences to new and unusual theatrical directions. Although an experienced stage director, he is best known for his film and TV roles.

"Doody" is an art teacher turned stripper turned creative dancer. Her recent autobiographical one-woman show, "A Parade to No Man's Land", was presented at the Universal Theatre.

A rehearsal of "Artaud at Rodez" at Melbourne's Pram Factory theatre. "The Pram", as it's known, was an old factory before becoming the headquarters for the Australian Performing Group. It is one of the most important workshop/theatres in the country.

▷
"Momma's Little Horror Show" at the Last Laugh Theatre Restaurant — a brilliantly devised performance employing mime, illusion and puppetry. Designed and directed by Nigel Triffitt, and performed by the Australian Puppet Theatre, it played to packed houses and was called by critics "a magical experience".

Victoria's economy— full of energy

by Sir Laurence Muir

One of Australia's leading financiers and businessmen, Laurie Muir these days regards himself as more of an "Australian" than a "Victorian". His home State, however, remains for him the "hub of the nation".

In this article, he sets the Victorian economy, past and present, into a national context; and does some crystal ball-gazing about future economic developments.

The Port of Melbourne is among the largest container ports in the world, handling more than half a million containers each year.

Victoria, the second smallest of the Australian States has, like its champion footballer, Leigh Matthews, always displayed an ability to position itself in the centre of things. Politically, economically, demographically and intellectually the State has long been the hub of the nation.

Its economic character was derived in three major stages — the gold rush of last century; the reticulation of cheap electricity from brown coal between the two world wars; and the discovery of vast oil and gas reserves in Bass Strait in the mid '60's.

Development of the State rushed forward in the middle of the 19th Century with the discovery of gold. As Geoffrey Dutton points out in his beautifully descriptive *Patterns of Australia*, "The gold rush that made 'marvellous Melbourne' also gave it a conscience. The Eureka Stockade, the gold miners' protest against Government interference has been Australia's only armed uprising. It was important both as symbol and as fact; the enormous influx of population and wealth following the gold rush created two contradictory strains of Victorians. On the one hand they became Australia's most sturdy and aggressive radicals. On the other they became Australia's greatest experts in the making and managing of money. Both strains were united in an allegiance to a 19th Century morality and took note of the moral tale available in the collapse of the great property boom towards the end of the century."

Despite the debacle of the 1890's Victoria emerged as the political and financial centre of Australia, and has tenaciously held on to her power and leadership in both areas, in spite of the rapid development of Sydney and Canberra.

For about 33 of the last 40 years a Victorian has been Australia's Prime Minister. The Stock Exchange of Melbourne retains a dominant position in the Australian securities industry. More than half of Australia's major companies have their headquarters in Melbourne.

With the gold rush came the brewing and engineering industries to Victoria.

The quest for gold and other minerals opened up the country, and the need to feed an expanding population soon demonstrated that Victoria possesses some of Australia's best sheep country (in the Western district), dairying land (in Gippsland and the north east) and wheatlands (in the Wimmera). Fruit and vegetables were intensively cultivated and extensive irrigation systems facilitated the development of a large canned and dried fruits industry.

Massive Energy Resources

Victoria achieved significant economic independence when in the Latrobe Valley one of the world's largest single deposits of brown coal was discovered, with reserves estimated at 100,000 million tonnes.

In 1919, the State Electricity Commission of Victoria was established under the leadership of Australia's Army Commander in World War One, Sir John Monash. The S.E.C.'s brief was to mine the brown coal, and to generate electricity and distribute it throughout the State.

Today the S.E.C. supplies virtually all the power needs of the State from the Yallourn-Morwell-Hazelwood complex where power is generated from thermal power stations fired by brown coal or briquettes. This abundant long term source is supplemented by peak load supplies of hydroelectric power from the Snowy Mountains Authority, gas turbines in the Latrobe Valley and the gas fired Newport Power Station in Melbourne.

As a boy growing up in the Latrobe Valley — locally always known simply as "the Valley" — in the '30's, I shared with my geology master many a discussion about potentials: the vast oil and gas fields that should be close to the brown coal deposits. Dr. Pritchard had no doubt they were there — "why, you can see the traces at Woodside. It must run out under Bass Strait," he'd say. "They'll find it in your lifetime".

I wish he'd been alive, that dear old man, when in 1965 the Barracouta natural gas field, and all that followed, was discovered by a joint venture between BHP and Esso — Victoria's (and Australia's) biggest company, in partnership with the world's biggest oil company.

Discoveries of oil and natural gas in Bass Strait have had an enormous impact on the economy of Victoria and Australia. The total initial reserves of 464 giga litres of oil and 220 giga cubic metres of gas make Victoria the most fortunate State in Australia in respect of petroleum reserves. A gas pipeline network will supply Melbourne and the main Victorian provincial cities with abundant natural gas for at least the next 30 years.

Thanks to Bass Strait's oil reserves and the potential for further discoveries Australia is almost 70% self sufficient in petroleum needs. Thanks to our energy resources overall (coal, oil, gas, uranium) Australia ranks second only to Norway among OECD countries in terms of exportable surplus of energy.

Taking Stock of the Present

To see the economic direction in which Victoria should be heading, we need first to take a closer look at the State's present situation.

Victoria has almost 30% of Australia's workforce and means of production and is committed to 35% of all manufacturing activity. Growth is assisted by political stability, and by the solid and consistent development of primary industry.

A look at the figures helps to put the State in perspective. Victoria accounts for 21% of total rural output, 75% of total butter output, 75% of dried fruits, 50% of cheese and 33% of potatoes. Victoria supplies about 20% of Australia's beef and veal exports and approximately 50% of the national mutton exports. The State has strong fishing and forest product industries. 81% of all motor vehicles manufactured in Australia are produced in Victoria, which is also the traditional home of the textile and footwear industries. Victoria shares with other States a soundly developed industrial base particularly in the fields of engineering, chemicals, food, paper, plastics and rubber.

Since the war, some $6 billion has been invested in Victoria by overseas interests — a third of the national total.

Victoria hosts one third of Australia's growing food and beverage industry, more than half of the textile and clothing industry and a third of the chemical industry. Traditionally Victoria has been the centre of Australia's aircraft manufacturing industry. Large packaging groups such as Australian Consolidated Industries, Australian Paper Manufacturers, J. Gadsden and Containers have major plants, and their headquarters, in Victoria. Melbourne is Australia's major general cargo port handling over 30% in value of the nation's trade. As such it is one of the world's leading container ports (moving more than 500,000 in a year).

The development of Tullamarine, Melbourne's International airport, over the last decade, has given tourism and commerce a major boost.

The State's service industries are well developed both in Melbourne and the regional centres. Banking, transportation and the media are especially strong. Newspapers such as The Age and The Herald, which go back almost to the very foundation of the colony of Victoria, have a high ranking amongst the great newspapers of the world.

The State Savings Bank of Victoria and the ANZ Banking Group have grown both in size and influence to positions of leadership in their respective sectors of the Australian banking industry.

Ansett, Trans Australia Airlines (TAA), Mayne Nickless, Thomas Nationwide Transport (TNT) and others continue to achieve dynamic growth in the transportation of goods and people. Tourism is growing rapidly thanks to good transportation, sound management, attractive climate and scenery. And for conventions, Melbourne has emerged as Australia's fastest growing centre, as a result of vigorous Government and private sector effort in recent years.

Retail sales in Victoria represent approximately 27% of the Australian total.

Gambling — and other Social Religions

Sport and gambling are growth industries in Australia, and Victoria plays a major role both in staging and participating in major sporting events.

Our home grown Australian Rules football is a big business, enjoying fanatical local attention during an ever-extending winter season.

Horse racing, betting and thoroughbred breeding are also big business.

The Melbourne Cup continues to hold its place as one of the world's major race classics. To borrow again from Geoff Dutton — "On the first Tuesday in November . . . even Sydney gives itself to Stately grey Melbourne. Moral Adelaide stops; the big North Terrace stores are deserted; in the chaste surroundings of the State library no one is looking at a book; staff and readers are gazing at a TV set hung from the ceiling. It is the same all over Australia. Church schools have a raffle on the Cup; the radio commands the silence of every pub drinker in Australia; everything is hushed by the incredible chant of the race commentator, somewhere between a Sung Eucharist and an orgasm. The horse in Australia has survived all the onslaughts of a mechanical age; surely few other countries in the world have a set of five postage stamps each with a famous horse on it."

Race track betting, the lottery and the TAB (Totalisator Agency Board, the official body running off-course betting) are substantial contributors to Government revenues. Victorians are keen participants in sporting events, both as players and onlookers. Melbourne stages major events such as an Olympic Games (1956), regular football finals, the Melbourne Cup and other classic horse meetings; the world's biggest crowds for Test Cricket, the autumn Moomba Carnival, super star concerts, and the annual Royal Melbourne Show. All of these are big business, with scope for growth.

In the post war period to the end of the 'seventies vigorous immigration policies attracted 5 million migrants to Australia: it is estimated that Victoria captured one third of this total. Immigration has been particularly important to Victoria, bringing new cultures, new customs, new energy, new products and new consumers. Victoria is now a truly homogeneous State with an exciting variety of tastes in food, clothing, music, homes, recreational and sporting activities.

Family formation and housing construction have benefited from the encouragement of new settlers. Many of the migrants who have been here for some time are very successful in business and are now leaders of cultural and public affairs. Many have sparked new business enterprises and have galvanised a more competitive Australian attitude and a higher productivity rate.

More recently our Asian migrants, especially from Vietnam, are starting to assimilate. They can be expected to contribute to a further broadening of Victorian culture and range of productive activities.

Charting a course for the Future

The challenge of the '80's for Victoria shows up in the declining prospects and prosperity of the main employment areas of the past. Japanese and other imported competition is rapidly diminishing the viability of local automobile manufacturing, textile and shoe industries, and is hurting many of the smaller industrial units which were sound in the past.

It is time for change. There is already much rationalisation under way. One problem now becoming apparent is that our mining and resource booms tend to be superimposed on, rather than integrated into, our economy.

In recent years, in contrast to many other nations, Australia's trade has failed to increase in proportion to Gross Domestic Product. Of course the US and Japanese economies have an even lower proportion than Australia, of trade to GDP. These countries, however, have a huge internal market with normally strong growth in consumer demand.

Australia (and Victoria) needs to concentrate on more rapid growth through immigration, which is the real power house of a strong internal consumer demand.

There is a need to find ways to spread the rewards of the resource boom evenly over the consumer economy.

Industries linked to investment (banking, mining, etc) and construction (steel, cement pipes, earth moving machinery, electrical equipment, transport, industrial instruments, heavy equipment) will experience strong demand in the '80's.

Victoria needs to press on quickly with the process of industry reconstruction, rationalisation and the development of new employment activities. As tariffs and quotas are reduced, the practical consideration of jobs and social repercussions make it most likely that the exchange rate mechanism will be used. Growth as a result will be limited by inflation management, bringing tight money and high interest rate policies to the fore.

The need for a larger and stronger internal consumer market will be felt increasingly as imported competition and overseas manufacturers limit our opportunities at home and abroad.

Thus the great challenge for Victoria's management for the 1980's is the enlargement of our employment opportunities so that three factors — growth in consumer demand, the enlargement of our internal consumption market and a strong immigration programme — become realities again.

Fortunately Australia's comparative energy advantage opens up new opportunities for the upgrading within Australia of our raw materials, farm products and the development of new energy intensive industries. The rash of new aluminium smelters and the huge plans for new petrochemical developments typify the new horizons.

Australia has once again an opportunity to expand its industrial base and to develop fresh employment opportunities by combining its abundant raw materials with its cheap energy prior to export. International investors have responded enthusiastically to the investment potential of energy rich Australia. The '80's have opened with the prospect of at least $2,000 million per annum of capital inflow for mining and industrial projects and portfolio investment. Australians are strong savers and our institutions are substantial and well organised.

The Australian capital market is well positioned to participate fully in funding the development needs of the next decade.

As one of the richest energy States, Victoria will be a major participant in these developments. Because of the State's highly skilled, well educated and diversified labour force, Victoria also has the raw material with which to find a place in the high technology industries now transforming the industrial world. Major employment opportunities exist in this area and an active partnership between Government and the private sector is essential to achieve rapid access and success.

One feature of Victoria which, apart from cheap energy, is assisting in the establishment here of new basic industries is the availability of several well equipped deep-water harbours. Aluminium smelting, oil refining and petrochemical industries are of special relevance in this context.

Looking Back — and Looking Forward

Victoria's history and development is studded with brilliant individual achievements. Each of us has our own list of these outstanding contributors. Some of the names which quickly come to my mind are:

Syme, Deakin, Isaacs, Monash, Menzies, McLennan, Bolte, Melba, Coles, Boyd, Grimwade, Dunlop, Coates, Dixon, Baillieu, Casey, Cowen, Myer, Murdoch, Nolan, Carnegie, Ansett, Hamer.

Such a list can never be complete, nor can it do justice to so many who deserve to be named. One thing seems clear: Victoria (and Australia) will continue to provide the atmosphere and stimulating environment for remarkable people (whether they be scientists, artists, entrepreneurs, industrialists, businessmen, educators, lawyers, politicians or without formal categorization) to emerge and contribute to the well being of others.

▷
Victoria's economic prosperity has traditionally been linked to the land.

Wishing and working upon a star

by R. D. Brown.

Professor Ron Brown is Chairman of the Chemistry Department at Monash University, Melbourne. A chemist turned astronomer, he, with his colleagues, is a world leader in pursuing new ideas of the origins of life.

Here he looks at the extraordinary range of current activity in technology and the sciences in Victoria, and examines some of its historical background.

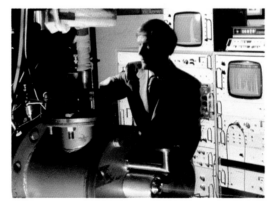

Victoria, and particularly its capital city Melbourne, lays claim to being the financial capital of the nation. But Victoria can also claim to be the major focus of science and technology in Australia. Over half of the nation's major industrial research laboratories are in and around the city of Melbourne, while scientific work based on universities and colleges also reaches its highest peak there. The Commonwealth Scientific and Industrial Research Organization (CSIRO) has many of its principal laboratories in Melbourne and in surrounding regions such as Geelong.

The reason for all of this scientific and technological achievement is partly rooted in the history of the State. The gold rushes of the 1850's brought to the infant colony a great influx of emigrants, many of whom were enterprising, talented and ambitious. From the wealth generated during the gold rush era, the great business houses developed in Melbourne and launched into a variety of industrial and technological enterprises.

With the gold rushes came many men of letters, responsible for the early start in Melbourne of such institutions as the National Museum, the Science Museum and the Royal Society of Victoria. The University of Melbourne also has its origins in the bustle of this prosperous period. Today there are four universities in and around Melbourne together with over forty other tertiary colleges and Institutes of Technology spread around Victoria. Scientific and technological activities in all of these tertiary institutions have well-established links with local industry, giving rise to many instances of fruitful collaboration in scientific investigation.

La Trobe University research has contributed to continuing improvements in Australian continental telecommunications; Melbourne University to useful new techniques for developing Australia's huge mineral resources. CSIRO has been closely associated, too, with the mining boom, and Monash University chemists are deeply involved in producing better results from Victoria's major supply of brown coal. Conversion of coal to oil figures prominently in a number of current vital research projects in the State. Marine research is also of fundamental importance: the Victorian Institute of Marine Sciences contributes significantly to scientific and industrial undertakings ranging from oil drilling to fisheries, and from weather forecasting to waste disposal.

Although institutions are of crucial importance to a growing community, progress ultimately depends on gifted individuals. Victoria has had a long history of clever people appearing at the right time. One early instance is James Harrison, editor of the Geelong Advertiser, who invented the world's first commercial refrigerator and patented it in 1856. By 1857 he had his refrigerator running on the banks of the Barwon River, turning out a ton of ice a day. Harrison's machine now resides in the Smithsonian Institute in Washington.

Throughout the 19th Century Melbourne maintained a lively interest in science and technology. Although Alexander Graham Bell's telephone first appeared in Boston in 1876 it was duplicated in Melbourne very soon after, with only the vaguest sketches for guidance. The telephone was working between commercial houses in Melbourne in 1878 and the city had its own telephone exchange by 1880.

Victorian scientists and engineers are continuing to effect historic technology. In the textile industry, for instance, the commercial spinning of wool had remained unchanged for nearly two hundred years. In 1764 an English spinner, James Hargreaves, noticing that an upright spindle continued to revolve when his small daughter accidentally knocked over his spinning wheel, had a flash of intuition that led to the invention of the spinning jenny. Jenny, from gin, or engine, increased the spinner's output eightfold and played a leading role in the industrial revolution.

The demise of the spinning jenny started in Geelong on February 8, 1961, when David Henshaw of the CSIRO Division of Textile Industry had the idea of a new kind of twist that could be imparted to yarn at a much faster rate.

Together with Gordon Walls he devised the principles of a new "self-twist" yarn machine. In due course the manufacturing firm of Repco Ltd. was brought into the project to produce prototype machines. Their team, under Lionel Stern, created a machine that surpassed anything seen in the textile industry. In February 1970 the world saw the first public demonstration of self-twist machines, spinning wool 12 times faster than ever before.

Recognition soon came in the form of the Prince Phillip Design Prize (1971) and the Encyclopaedia Britannica Australia Award for Science (1972). More than 1600 machines worth $A15 million have now been exported. The further development of the basic idea has steadily continued. In 1975 the third generation of machine was unveiled — the SELFIL spinner. This produces a completely new type of yarn from a mixture of wool and synthetics, spinning at 16 times the speed of conventional machines.

Victorian textile scientists and technologists have produced a world-wide winner whose impact is still being felt. They've certainly produced a new twist to an old yarn!

Stargazing

Professor Keith Cole is a space scientist who works in Upper Atmosphere Physics. His group at La Trobe University is engaged in the experimental and theoretical study of the ionosphere and the magnetosphere. Although this work is essentially pure science, the results are likely to be of considerable practical importance in such areas as radio communication, because the ionosphere reflects radiowaves around the Earth.

This work by Professor Cole and his colleagues is internationally celebrated. He is a member of a U.S. team based at the NASA/Goddard Space Flight Centre in Greenbelt, Maryland, studying properties of the magnetosphere using the Dynamics Explorer Satellite. Another joint program involves members of the Institute of Physics of the Earth in Moscow, while most members of his group have been involved in programs of upper atmosphere research in Antarctica.

Stargazing to the past, for the future

My own team studies chemical processes that occur out in space where new planetary systems will form — work which takes us to some of the world's most sensitive radio telescopes: at Parkes in New South Wales; at Kitt Peak in Arizona, U.S.A.; and Onsala in Sweden. We are finding evidence of the precursors of life molecules in space. Onsala's 20-metre telescope dish is 'smoother' than Parkes' giant 64-metre dish, and enables us to read radio waves as short as 1mm.

The very weak signals coming from chemical clouds in space are molecular 'fingerprints' that first have to be measured in the laboratory. Monash University laboratories are fully equipped with the highly sensitive microwave and millimetre wave instruments needed for the fundamental studies of the 'fingerprints'. The labs, at Clayton, are contributing further parts to the jigsaw which, when complete, may answer the question as to whether life as we know it originated in space or here on planet Earth.

"State of the art" equipment and knowledge in such specialized high technology — an invaluable national resource — includes digital computers, vacuum tanks, cryogenics and lasers, the latter used to study elusive charged molecules from the space clouds. The charged molecules repel one another, making incredibly difficult the task of reading their signals.

At Monash we have now perfected the technique of producing 'fingerprints' of charged particles in space, making the University the world centre for space spectroscopy of molecules. We may now have the key to an understanding of how planets are formed.

Much nearer to home — reading the mineral boom

Victorian scientists have made many discoveries to solve problems that arise in the hot, hard slog of Australia's vital mineral industries. One important new invention overcomes the difficult task of measuring how the various mineral constituents of an ore are distributed, how they are associated, and especially how they are distributed after the ore has been crushed and ground to liberate the minerals. For commercial purposes it is impractical to conduct extensive microscopic examinations; the miners needed something more efficient, systematic — and preferably automatic.

Dr. Alan Reid of the CSIRO Division of Mineral Chemistry developed an extraordinary system called QEM * SEM, for Quantitative Evaluation of Minerals by Scanning Electron Microscopy. A commercial prototype is now operational and an Australian company, E.T.P., has been licenced to manufacture and market QEM * SEM: almost certainly another winner for the ingenious and practical Victorian scientists in CSIRO.

The Basics: Coal and Oil

Victoria has very large quantities of easily recoverable brown coal, raising the attractive possibility — for a country a long way from Middle East oilfields — of converting some of the coal into liquid fuels. Brown coal has specific chemical and physical properties that are advantageous for the conversion process. Victorian scientists have been quick to help in the investigation of how to achieve optimal conversion. Professor Siemon and Dr. Yost in the Department of Chemical Engineering at Melbourne University are investigating the reaction of carbon monoxide with wet coal as a cheaper alternative to the established reaction of dried coal with hydrogen.

A joint programme of research between the Departments of Chemistry and Chemical Engineering at Monash University, directed by Associate Professor J. B. Agnew, Professor W. R. Jackson and Dr. F. P. Larkins, is developing new catalytic systems for the reaction of coal slurries in suitable solvents. High conversions of coal into liquids can be achieved using catalytic systems based mainly on cheap iron-containing materials together with a very small amount of the more expensive metal, tin.

Broken Hill Proprietary Research Laboratories in Clayton also have facilities for studying the hydrogenation of coal. A team led by Dr. Noam White is mainly working with coals of higher grade from New South Wales, but much of their work will be applied to conversion of Victorian coals.

Victoria's laboratories are making a leading contribution to Australia's research effort in the coal conversion area and this may be the first State to have a commercial plant — operating as a result of local research effort coupled with technological expertise from overseas.

Combining Rock and Stars

The popular image of a geology department is of a building fitted out with showcases full of rock samples and mineral specimens, especially relating to the nearby countryside. The Geology Department at Melbourne University is a much more exotic place, thanks to the skill and imagination of Professor John Lovering. His international reputation is based on his geological studies of rocks coming from far greater distances — meteorites from space.

Not surprisingly he was one of the select band of scientists chosen by NASA (the USA's National Aeronautic and Space Administration) to study the moon rocks brought back in 1969 from the historic Apollo 11 manned lunar landing. One of his discoveries was of an entirely new mineral, Tranquillityite — named after the lunar landing site on the Sea of Tranquillity.

Turning from space science to earth science, Professor Lovering set up a research group studying fission tracks — microscopic tracks produced in minerals when uranium atoms undergo atomic fission. There appears to be a number of valuable applications derivable from the study of fission tracks, from determining the ages of mineral samples and the study of continental drift, to the measurement of the thermal history of rocks — the latter being of great potential economic importance in the search for oil. With new uses for the fission track technique being discovered by Professor Lovering's group almost monthly, it is an exciting time to be a "fission tracker" in Victoria!

CSIRO's QEM*SEM — a speedy way of scanning minerals.

Coal to oil at Monash University — testing the tubular reactor for gas leaks.

Professor John Lovering of Melbourne University — discoverer of a new moon mineral.

SGE has received three export awards for specialised precision scientific equipment. It employs more than 100 people.

Queenscliff Marine Science Laboratories — sampling for phytoplankton, the most sensitive indicator of heavy metal and nutrient pollution.

High Technology in Glass

One of Australia's greatest success stories in high technology and the capturing of major overseas markets surrounds Ernest Dawes, Managing Director of Scientific Glass Engineering (SGE Pty. Ltd.).

Starting as a scientific glass technician, first at Melbourne University and then at the research laboratories of I.C.I.A.N.Z., he recognised the central role played by precision glass syringes and micro-syringes in modern science. The unique and elegantly simple methods of manufacture that he devised when he struck out on his own in 1966 enabled him to build up a thriving company with an outstanding overseas export performance.

Biology's contribution

Two major biological research projects at Melbourne universities have direct industrial implications.

Professor A. B. Wardrop's elucidation of the structure of cell walls in wood has revealed broad correlations between cell structure in raw timber and related qualities of strength, shrinkage and swelling in pulp and paper. His work, at CSIRO and now at La Trobe University, should significantly decrease waste in the forestry industry.

Professor Bruce Holloway, of the Genetics Department at Monash, is working with micro-organisms of importance to medicine, agriculture and industry.

By using naturally occurring genetic processes, improved strains of bacteria are being developed for use in biotechnology. His current projects include research on the production of bacterial protein as an animal feed, and on bacterial strains which can efficiently leach mineral ores.

Bounty from the Sea

Australia is a remote island continent at the junction of the Pacific, Southern and Indian Oceans. Because of its location it has always had a major interest in the oceans, but in recent years its marine resources and environment have assumed even greater importance.

Some of the developments that illustrate the increasing significance of our marine environment are: offshore petroleum exploration and exploitation; more effective technologies for fisheries and transportation; intensive use of coasts and offshore areas for recreation; new techniques of climatic prediction and control; and the recognition of opportunities for economic and efficient waste disposal.

The declaration of the 200 nautical mile exclusive economic zone in 1979 provides additional responsibilities and opportunities, and requires Australia to give increasing recognition to the importance of the seas.

To develop and manage its marine resources effectively this continental nation faces an exciting scientific and technological challenge. The Victorian Institute of Marine Sciences (VIMS) is helping Australia to meet that challenge.

VIMS is based at the Marine Sciences Laboratories of the Ministry for Conservation at Queenscliff, on Port Phillip Bay. The VIMS Act of 1974 provides the Institute with scientific autonomy.

Financed by both government and private sources, VIMS is directed by a Council that includes many of Australia's most celebrated scientists. Its small permanent staff has access to a wide range of scientists and engineers with specialist skills to help it tackle the diverse and exciting problems of the waters around the Victorian coast. VIMS' main interest is currently focussed on Bass Strait, attempting to develop an understanding of the fundamental processes that drive this complex marine system. Improvements in harvesting such an economically vital region of Australia's continental shelf may well emerge, thanks to the skilled scientific initiatives of VIMS.

In the past and in the present, wishing for a better future — and working hard for it — has been characteristic of both research and industry in Victoria. Initiatives in science and technology are now helping to shape Victoria's future: from the depths of Bass Strait, through slurries of brown coal, and out to the stars.

Science and the economy

Health for all — dream or reality?

by Sir Gustav Nossal
Director of the Walter and Eliza Hall
Institute of Medical Research, Melbourne.

New approaches to some of mankind's most dreaded diseases are being developed in Victoria. In this article, the world-renowned immunologist Sir Gustav Nossal discusses some of the promising new methods being studied at Victoria's three major Institutes of Medical Research.

Good health! A greeting that rings out in all languages to express one of mankind's most cherished hopes. Good health throughout life to a hale old age is a worthwhile dream for everyone — but how can it be translated into reality?

In this article, we shall range over subjects as diverse as the fight against leukaemia; control over such tropical diseases as malaria; development of new vaccines; the "cloning" of the body's soldiers, the white blood cells, to wage war against cancer; new approaches to heart disease and high blood pressure; novel hormones and how they can help in health or disease.

Victoria has led Australia in medical research over many years. Its distinguished tradition owes much to giants of earlier years. Among the triumphs are Kate Campbell's classic discovery that too much oxygen can cause blindness in premature babies; Charles Kellaway's work on snake venoms and anti-venenes; John Cade's revolutionary finding that lithium can control serious mental disorders; and Macfarlane Burnet's pioneering techniques for the growth and study of viruses outside the living body, essential prerequisites for the development of vaccines such as those against poliomyelitis or measles.

Still, so much remains to be done. Our ability to prevent or cure some chronic diseases is incomplete, because medical research has not yet revealed enough about what actually causes them. This is where the future lies. Only medical research can unlock the secrets and pave the way to more rational control measures. If the past is any guide at all to the future, then medical research represents more than an act of faith. It is a vital national investment.

Victoria's Place in World Medical Research

Victorians realised early on that the professional pursuit of first class medical research requires an appropriate institutional framework. The oldest, and by now the largest, of its medical research institutes, The Walter and Eliza Hall Institute of Medical Research, was founded in 1916. It is affiliated with The Royal Melbourne Hospital and The University of Melbourne, and employs about 200 people including 70 scientists. The Baker Medical Research Institute and The Howard Florey Institute of Experimental Physiology and Medicine are also world-renowned. Distinguished research is performed in all the major hospitals, both in smaller private medical research institutes attached to them, such as those at Prince Henry's Hospital, St. Vincent's Hospital and The Royal Children's Hospital; and by academics in university medical schools. The Victorian State Government runs two important establishments, the Cancer Research Institute attached to the Peter McCallum Clinic and the Mental Health Research Institute. I could also list a number of Commonwealth laboratories for which Victoria is the host, and it would be impossible to do justice to all the Victorians engaged in the great humanitarian adventure of medical research. For this reason, I have decided to concentrate on the work I know best, namely that of the Hall Institute.

Immunology — A New Major Branch of Medicine

For most of us, immunology means no more than the familiar triple-antigen shots and polio vaccines we give our children. But the study of the body's own defence system has moved on from simple immunisation techniques to embrace many of the most exciting areas of internal medicine, such as cancer, organ transplants and auto immune diseases. This is the new immunology which has been the Hall Institute's chief field of interest for more than 20 years.

The central star in the drama of the new immunology is a cell called the lymphocyte. This small, innocuous-looking white blood cell has long been known as a major weapon in the fight against infectious diseases. When a foreign microbe enters the body, or when a vaccination procedure mimics the process, the lymphocytes are provoked into strenuous activity. They become much larger and multiply, each developing a complex internal 'factory' to mass-produce powerful germ-fighting proteins — the antibody molecules.

The new thrust in immunology research is concerned with three other things that lymphocytes can do: to mount a "search and destroy" mission against cancer; to foil the surgeon's triumphs in organ transplantation; and to turn rebel and create civil warfare in the body.

Starting a "Palace Revolution"

It now seems likely that the body's own defence systems can be harnessed to fight cancer. If we can master the techniques involved, we will have a major new weapon against man's most dreaded disease.

The secret of this defence system lies in the lymphocytes, which constantly patrol the body looking for trouble, like policemen on the beat. These cells know only one thing — how to recognise material foreign to the body ("non-self") from the body's own constituents ("self"). Some pre-cancerous growths and some actual malignant cancers show molecules on their surface that are recognizably different from those on normal cells. In living animals, it is probable that lymphocytes are all the time locating and destroying cells where certain pre-malignant changes are evident, thereby keeping the tissues healthy and clean. Cancers may represent cells that, by one trick or another, have escaped detection.

The Hall Institute is working to find ways to increase the lymphocyte 'police force' and so strengthen the body's own natural defence against cancer.

Spare Parts Surgery: Kidney Grafts and Other Organ Transplants

The same lymphocytes that fight microbes and cancer cells can be a medical hazard when surgeons transplant organs such as the kidney. They invade the new kidney, which they see as foreign, and destroy it. In this case, we have to use strong drugs to subdue the immune attack and the present, better than 75 per cent, success rate of kidney transplants shows how much progress has been made.

This evident success in kidney transplantation whets the appetite for organ replacement in other diseases. Some groups are achieving a notable percentage of successes in the transplantation of organs such as the heart or the liver.

At the Hall Institute, we have developed a special interest in certain cells of the pancreas gland that manufacture insulin. We believe that if the transplant barrier can be overcome, a graft of insulin-secreting human cells would represent much more sensible treatment of diabetes than a lifetime of insulin injections.

We are investigating special techniques of tissue culture that would allow us to transplant these pancreas cells without alerting the lymphocyte defences.

The 'Civil War' Diseases: Autoimmunity in the Body

Sometimes the lymphocyte's "self-non-self" discrimination breaks down, and then serious disease can result. The lymphocyte turns traitor and begins to manufacture antibodies against some component of the body itself, such as the kidney, liver or an endocrine gland. This dreadful civil warfare in the body is called autoimmune disease. Far from being an exotic rarity, autoimmune processes are involved in diseases as important and common as diabetes, Bright's disease, cirrhosis of the liver and multiple sclerosis.

Let us consider one or two examples. When a young, newly-diagnosed diabetic first enters the clinic, it is common to find that he or she has antibodies in the blood-stream that are specific for just those very cells in the pancreas that are capable of synthesizing insulin. The antibodies are destroying the insulin-producing cells. Once these cells are gone, the antibodies often disappear, but then it is too late. The cells cannot be regenerated, and the patient is diabetic for life. Certain examples of Bright's disease are equally instructive.

There is a portion of the blood filtration mechanism of the kidney, called the basement membrane, which is absolutely vital for the correct production of urine. Sometimes the lymphocytes make antibodies against kidney basement membrane, and the filters are gummed up to such an extent that the kidney fails.

In order to treat autoimmune disease, there are only two pathways open. Either we must replace the vital substance no longer being produced — and this is how we cope today with diabetes, pernicious anaemia or thyroid failure — or we must shut off the production of the bad antibodies by drugs. This drug stratagem is working successfully in diseases such as lupus and chronic hepatitis.

Antibodies and Genetic Engineering

The antibodies made following an infection or a vaccination are highly specific. Measles vaccination protects you against measles, not polio, and *vice versa*. How can the human body make the vast array of different antibodies needed to protect us against the large number of different organisms present in our environment? Genetic engineering technology is giving us the answers, and the Molecular Biology Laboratory of the Hall Institute, under Dr. J. M. Adams, has been prominently involved.

Genetic engineering (or recombinant DNA technology) permits the study of human or animal genes. The genes are the coded blue-prints or instructions lying in the nucleus of each cell which tell the cell what to do and how to do it. Genes are inherited equally from father and mother, but as a complex, random mixture permitting many fascinating new combinations and variations in each human being.

In a recombinant DNA experiment, a gene can be snipped out of its proper setting in the nucleus, spliced into a piece of bacterial gene, and replicated many times, so making enough of the particular gene to allow analysis by chemistry.

As a result, we now know that each person has the inherited, genetic capacity to make about 50,000 different antibodies, and that mutations take place within the lymphocytes during life, expanding this repertoire of antibody types to at least 10 million, and probably more.

Cell Cloning: How to Harness Cancer Cells to Useful Purposes

Many of these precious antibodies can now be made in the test tube by the hybridoma method. Currently of enormous value in research, the hybridoma antibodies in the future will find a brilliant place both in diagnosis and treatment of disease.

The way in which the hybridoma technique works is both simple and ingenious. Healthy cells, such as antibody-forming cells, perform specialised functions but have a finite life-span. Cancer cells frequently have forgotten what the normal cell, from which they arose, used to do, but have learnt the trick of immortality — while appropriate nutrition is provided, they just keep on dividing. In the hybridoma technique, a cancer cell is fused with a normal antibody-producing cell, in much the same manner as a child may push two globules of mercury together to make a bigger globule. This fused cell sometimes manages to grow like the cancerous parent, but make antibody like the healthy parent — thus providing a virtually limitless source of the precious, highly pure antibody molecules.

Cloning Specific Warriors: Anti-Cancer Lymphocytes

The lymphocytes are being used in the Hall Institute in another, entirely new way to fight cancer. This is by "cloning" or duplicating these warrior cells.

In Australia, the strong sunlight acting on the rather light skins inherited from British and other Northern European forebears, causes a high incidence of skin cancer. Most of these skin cancers are easily cured, but one variety, the black pigmented mole known as malignant melanoma, can be fatal unless caught early. Australia (and particularly Queensland and Western Australia) has the highest frequency of fatal melanoma in the world, a fact that is all the more distressing because so many victims are young or in the prime of life.

In the Clinical Research Unit of the Institute under Dr. I. R. Mackay, a laboratory devoted to cancer research is funded by the Anti-Cancer Council of

Victoria as a result of the generosity of members of the Lions' Club. Here, Dr. G. Burns is exploring a novel approach to melanoma. He found that many of the tumours have been infiltrated by lymphocytes. As a working hypothesis, it is believed that these may be in the active process of trying to kill the tumour, though clearly the effort is too feeble.

What would happen if each of these little soldiers could be "cloned" and thereby replicated 1,000-fold? This is precisely the aim of our research. The lymphocytes are separated away from the malignant cells and treated with special growth hormones so that they multiply in the test tube. Eventually the hope is to re-inject these "cloned" cells back into the patient, so that the now much stronger army can fight the cancer.

Vaccines for Third World Diseases

While thousands of millions of dollars are spent worldwide in the search for better health for the affluent developed nations, whole populations in the less developed countries are still threatened by tropical parasitic diseases like malaria and schistosomiasis or snail fever. Vaccines to prevent transmissible diseases represent history's most cost-effective public health tool — as the war against smallpox has shown — yet no vaccine has yet been produced for malaria or any other human parasitic disease.

The Immunoparasitology Laboratory of the Hall Institute, under Dr. G. F. Mitchell, has launched a three-fold programme of research, aimed at the better understanding of immune responses against parasites; the development of vaccines, especially against malaria; and at quicker, cheaper diagnostic tests for these diseases. In this research, valuable linkages have been formed with laboratories in Papua-New Guinea and the Philippines. The research is strongly supported by the World Health Organisation and the Rockefeller Foundation. Vaccines against parasites will not be easy to produce. In many cases, the parasite has evolved mechanisms over millions of years to evade the natural immune defences of the host. Yet we believe each parasite must have an Achilles' heel. We are seeking to be cleverer still than the parasite, trapping it at the weakest point of its life cycle. Tests with animals suggest we are on the threshold of success.

This is only a part of the story of the Hall Institute. There are many other threads which could be pursued. So that our work may flourish well into the 21st Century, the State Government of Victoria is joining with the Commonwealth Government of Australia to sponsor a total rebuilding of the Institute on The Royal Melbourne Hospital site. This $30 million project is timed for completion in late 1984, and we hope the opening will form a significant part of that year's sesquicentenary celebrations for the founding of Victoria.

The Baker Medical Research Institute

The Baker Medical Research Institute is the only institute in Australia devoted entirely to the study of heart disease. It was founded in 1926 by Thomas Baker, a Melbourne businessman, and now has a staff of 120. Its affiliations are with the Alfred Hospital and Monash University.

The Institute works to discover the causes of high blood pressure and atherosclerosis, which produce strokes and heart attacks and together account for over 50% of all deaths in Australia. Its research program looks at the mechanisms which control blood pressure, blood fats and the nutrition of arteries. The aim is to develop new approaches which might delay or even prevent the onset of high blood pressure and heart attacks.

In a normal person, the level of the blood pressure depends on how much blood the heart is pumping (cardiac output) and on the resistance of blood flow offered by the small arteries. Blood pressure becomes high due to an increase in one or other of these factors. One aspect of the Institute's research is to investigate the role of the kidney and its hormones on fluid balance disturbances, which are the main long-term causes of high cardiac output. Another line of research relates to the search for "constrictor" factors which increase

resistance to the blood flow of the arteries; as part of this work, new biochemical techniques have been developed to explore the role of "stress" as a cause of high blood pressure. With the new techniques developed at the Institute, we should soon be able to determine which of the many causes of high blood pressure are present in individual patients.

The Baker Institute has the only Cardiovascular Surgical Research Unit in Australia. Some of this research is very "applied" — how to protect the heart from trauma and damage during open heart surgery. Because of the ready availability of the Institute's facilities in the basic sciences, it has been relatively easy to determine to what temperature the heart should be cooled and the composition of the liquid in which it should be bathed. This new knowledge is critically important in making these major surgical procedures safer and better.

The Howard Florey Institute.

The Howard Florey Institute of Experimental Physiology and Medicine, one of the world's leading medical centres, is affiliated with the University of Melbourne. Established some 30 years ago, the Institute specialises in endocrinology (the study of hormones) and the brain mechanisms underlying instinctive behaviour. The two areas overlap since hormones have a major effect on behaviour patterns and, conversely, brain states such as emotion, anxiety or fear may have profound effects on hormone secretion.

An initial interest was the salt-retaining hormone of the adrenal gland called aldosterone. This hormone is implicated in important disease states such as dropsy of heart, kidney and liver disease, and in high blood pressure. Finding out how it was controlled physiologically was crucial to understanding its role in disease; but the adrenal gland is sited deep in the abdomen and is not easily studied.

The Institute research teams devised a way of transplanting the adrenal gland from the abdomen of a sheep to a specially-constructed skin pouch in its

neck, using original plastic and vascular surgical techniques. The large neck skin folds of the Merino sheep were ideal for this method. At the same time, crucial advances were made in procedures for measuring aldosterone. These procedures led to the discovery of major new information on how the adrenal gland is controlled, and the method was a landmark in experimental endocrinology. It has since been applied to the study of the ovary and uterus, thyroid, parathyroid, kidney and pancreas.

The Institute is also investigating hormones produced by the pituitary gland, the ovary, kidney and parathyroid glands. Hormones from these organs govern a number of vital processes, and one under particular study is the ovarian hormone 'relaxin' which controls the normal birth processes. Recently the research teams have cloned the gene for relaxin and determined its chemical structure. The studies on this and other reproductive hormones aim at important advances in the prevention of birth injury (which accounts for some 50% of spastic and cerebral palsy children), better fertility control and the treatment of arthritis.

The analysis of instinctual behaviour, especially appetite, also has medical relevance. Many people see the doctor because of underlying emotional and mental problems, rather than immediate organic disease. Research on the basic brain processes involved in thirst, hunger, sexual and maternal behaviour, and other body functions, is shedding new light on such problems as anorexia nervosa, obesity, hypertension, depression and anxiety, alcoholism and addictive behaviours.

Conclusion

This brief chapter presents just the tip of the iceberg of Victoria's medical research. I must emphasise again the vital importance of university-based research, strong in its own right and inextricably intertwined with the universities' educational mission. It can truly be said that Victoria's medical researchers are a force to be reckoned with in international circles, and they are among the best ambassadors for Australia.

Science and the economy.
Photography by Ian McKenzie.

Major discoveries of natural gas (1965) and oil (1967) have been made in Bass Strait. These reserves have been developed jointly by Esso — B.H.P. at a cost, so far, of over $1,200 million. The six wells already operating provide more than 70% of Australia's crude oil requirements, and exploration is underway elsewhere along the Victorian coast to locate new fields. Known reserves are expected to meet Australia's needs well into the 1990's.

Compared with oil from the Middle East, Bass Strait crude is light and well-suited for the production of transport fuels, including motor-spirit, distillate and avgas.

Two rigs now operating in Bass Strait produce both gas and oil: TUNA, and BARRACOUTA, the closest to shore, some 25 kilometres off the Gippsland coast south-east of Sale. Four more — HALIBUT, KINGFISH A & B, and MACKEREL, the biggest, in a depth of 93 metres — produce oil; and one, MARLIN, produces gas. The design of the rigs ensures that the structures are capable of withstanding the force of a "100 year wave" for Bass Strait — i.e. the most powerful wave likely to occur in the area once in a hundred years — a monster estimated at 18 metres from trough to crest. Bass Strait is violent water, subject to frequent storms, and transport to and from rigs is primarily by helicopter. Project expediture through to 1986 has been authorised at $468 million, including construction of five more platforms.

A new gas rig, SNAPPER, is in the water, and two more oil rigs, COBIA and WEST KINGFISH are pictured on the slipways at Barry Beach Marine Terminal at Corner Inlet, 200 kilometres south-east of Melbourne. Two others, FORTESCUE and FLOUNDER — the biggest yet to be built in Australia — are in the early stages of construction. Because of its isolation, construction materials are brought into Barry Beach by boat.

Victoria's Latrobe Valley contains one of the world's largest single deposits of brown coal, with reserves estimated at 100,000 million tonnes. The State Electricity Commission mines the coal in huge open-cuts, burns it in a series of power stations, and distributes electricity throughout the State. This abundant long-term source is supplemented by peak-load supplies of hydroelectric power from the Snowy Mountains Authority, gas turbines in the Latrobe Valley and the gas-fired Newport Power Station in Melbourne.

These pictures, at the Morwell open cut, show the vast extent of the coal reserves.

The huge bucket-wheel dredges work 24 hours a day, operating under floodlights at night.

In the early morning, the coal face is sometimes shrouded in mist, lending an eerie quality to the scene.

Victoria's newest power station complex is under construction at Loy Yang, near Morwell. The State's biggest bucket-wheel dredge is being built on paddocks which soon will turn from green to the black/brown of an open cut mine. As long as goal-to-goal on the M.C.G., the Loy Yang super-dredge is twice as big as any previously built (nearly 200 metres) and can take 60,000 tonnes of coal per day.

A huge bunker to store coal for the power station is being built, and enormous concrete slabs are being swung into place, interlocking like a child's construction kit.

The first unit at Loy Yang is due to come on-stream in the mid 1980's.

113

Petrochemicals are one of Victoria's major industries, representing nearly half the current Australia-wide annual capital investment of $1,432 million, and employing nearly five thousand people.

The biggest plants are at Altona (Petroleum Refineries of Australia, a Mobil/Esso project opened in 1949, the first refinery in Australia); Westernport (B.P. Australia); and Geelong (Shell Australia — where these pictures were taken).

The Shell petrochemical plant at Geelong, the biggest in Victoria and second biggest in Australia, has been operating since 1954. Capability is 132,000 barrels per stream-day, manufacturing a total of over 5 million tonnes of petrochemical product a year. Pictures include the main catalytic cracker, glittering with lights at dusk; a central control room; and part of the tank farm which can store 1,052 megalitres — a third of Victoria's storage capacity.

Oil and gas from the Bass Strait oilfields are piped directly to the refineries. A small amount of more viscous Mid-East crude is brought in by tanker for heavy fuel-oil usage. Victoria is fortunate in having excellent deep-water ports at Westernport, Melbourne, Geelong and Portland. On Westernport, about 70 kilometres from Melbourne, the Long Island Point Fractionation Plant receives stabilized crude oil, L.P.G. and ethane from Longford — 189 kilometres of pipeline away — where Bass Strait oil and gas come ashore. Ethane is used as a feedstock to the petrochemical industry for the manufacture of ethylene and styrene monomer. In turn these products are used to make polyethylene plastic (food wraps, plastic bags), and polystyrene foam (surf boards, packaging, insulation and much else). Other products made from ethylene in Victoria include synthetic rubber (for tyres), insecticides, solvents, refrigerant, antifreeze, explosives, detergents, brake fluid, synthetic fibres like Orlon and Dacron, lubricants and adhesives.

Fishing has been developing rapidly in Victoria in recent years, and several important new fishing grounds have been located. There are two dozen fishing ports in Victoria, with major centres at Lakes Entrance, Portland and San Remo. Some 200 boats regularly go to sea, to catch crayfish (mainly exported to the US as frozen lobster tails), scallops, abalone, shark and a variety of trawlfish. Jigging for squid is also being developed, as a joint venture between Australia and Japan. Fish stocks are protected by strict fisheries regulations.

Victoria's favourite fish — found everywhere in the State's Fish and Chip shops — is "flake", the local name for fillets from small shark. Among the newer species rising in popularity are John Dory, Blue Grenadier and Gemfish.

▷
The "Aqua Enterprise", a modern and well-equipped Stern Trawler from Port Fairy, with owner Paul Armstrong. There is good money to be made from fishing, and many young people are now entering the industry. Catch on 'Aqua Enterprise' includes Blue Grenadier, Gemfish and John Dory.

◁
Looking serene against the night sky is "Halcyon", one of the Portland trawlers fishing for Gemfish, Blue Grenadier and John Dory, in the recently opened trawling grounds south of Portland.

▷ (far right)
Crew of the "Delphinus", the ocean-going Fisheries Patrol Vessel of the Fisheries and Wildlife Division, using radar to locate a fishing fleet.

▽
Albatross and other seabirds follow the fishing boats, snapping up any fish waste thrown overboard.

Aluminium smelting, with its heavy demand for electricity, is one of many industries in Victoria taking advantage of power from the vast Latrobe Valley coalfields. This is the Alcoa smelter at Geelong, which processes alumina brought in by sea from Western Australia. Alcoa is currently building a $415 million smelter at Portland, due to start production in July, 1983.

Vehicle-building has traditionally been important in Victoria: Australia's "own" car, the Holden, was developed here. This is the General Motors — Holden plant at Dandenong. GMH, like Ford, Nissan, Toyota and other major car companies, are developing the 'world car' concept which will greatly change the international car scene.

Melbourne has traditionally been the financial capital of Australia. Many of the largest financial institutions have their headquarters here, as do a good many of Australia's biggest companies.

At the city's financial heart is the Stock Exchange of Melbourne, where on average more than $11 million in stocks and shares change hands every day.

Melbourne is also the centre of medical research in Australia, and offers world-class facilities at both public and private hospitals. Major public hospitals include the Alfred (a major centre for open-heart surgery), Queen Victoria (where Australia's test tube baby program began), St. Vincent's, Prince Henry's, the Royal Melbourne, and the Austin (Melbourne's main hospital for spinal injuries).

▷

World-class facilities for babies and children are provided at the Royal Melbourne Children's Hospital (shown here in three photos), the most extensive pediatric hospital in the Southern Hemisphere. The Royal Children's has a celebrated programme in basic clinical research and is noted for its pioneering achievements in children's cardiac surgery.

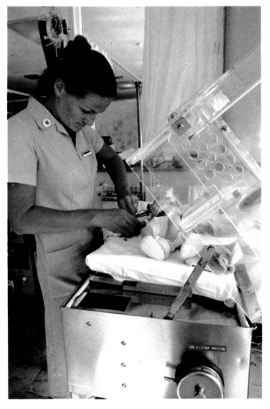

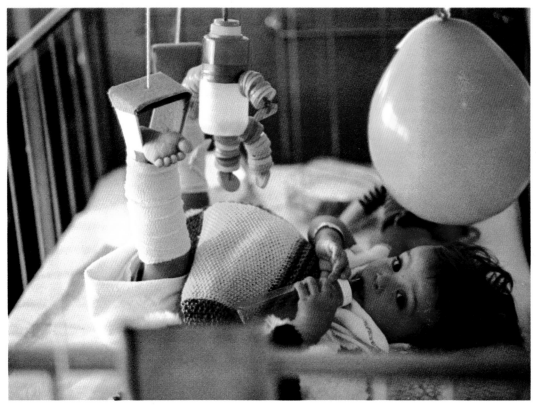

One of the programs at the Walter and Eliza Hall Institute for Medical Research (photo above) seeks to develop vaccines against malaria and other tropical parasitic diseases. A number of researchers from Third World countries are working on the program in Melbourne, under the direction of Dr. G. F. Mitchell.

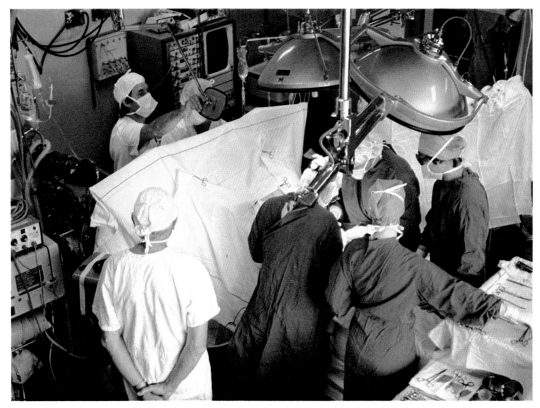

Since the first breweries began in Melbourne in Little Collins Street in 1851, glass-making has been an important Victorian industry. Beer bottles are an essential part of quenching Victoria's thirst, and many millions are manufactured at this A.C.I. plant in a total production of over 700 million glass containers per year. Recycling is important, and some 30,000 tonnes of cullet (or broken glass) is reprocessed in Victoria every year.

Trees cover a third of Victoria — some seven million hectares. About 30% of the forest is managed by the Forests Commission, largely for sawlogs and pulpwood, forest recreation and catchment protection. In addition, there are extensive privately-owned plantations, mainly of soft-woods such as *pinus radiata*. Australian Paper Manufacturers, at its Maryvale Mill, produces annually nearly half a million tonnes of kraft paper and packaging materials, mainly using soft-woods from its own forests. Native hardwoods such as Mountain Ash and other eucalypts are used mainly for sawn timber, although some is used for pulp and paper.

Fishermen's Bend, Victoria has been the centre of the Australian aircraft manufacturing industry since 1936. Two major aircraft manufacturers — the Government Aircraft Factories and the Commonwealth Aircraft Corporation — have their plants there.

◁
The Commonwealth Aircraft Corporation, a private company in which B.H.P. and Rolls-Royce are major shareholders, designed and manufactured the mechanical elements in the Barra sonar buoy, seen here in C.A.C.'s hydrodynamic test-tank. Now in world-wide use, the Barra's brilliantly innovative electronics were designed in Australia by A.W.A.

The C.A.C. repairs and overhauls the ATAR 9C engine of the Mirage fighter, and the Viper engines of Macchi jet trainers.

▷
G.A.F. employs 1,500 at Fishermen's Bend, and another 450 at Avalon airfield, near Geelong.

The Jindivick target drone is also under production at G.A.F. The Jindivick is ground controlled and is used during practice manoevres for target training.

The famous Nomad STOL aircraft is made by G.A.F. Capable of take-off on an incredibly short 400-metre runway, the Nomad has penetrated the hugely competitive aircraft market in North America, becoming one of the most popular small commuter craft sold for commercial purposes in the US.

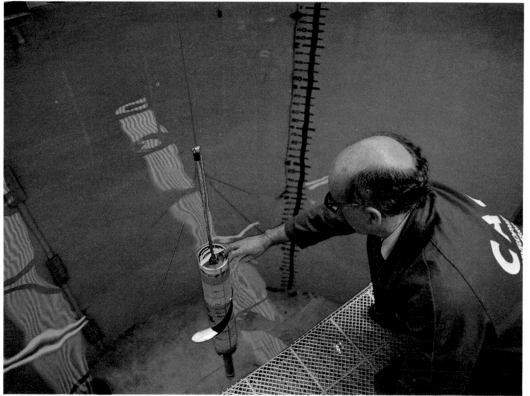

126

Biographies

Phillip Adams

Phillip Adams was born in Maryborough, Victoria, in 1939. He is the author of a number of best-selling books, including "Adams With Added Enzymes", "The Unspeakable Adams" and "More Unspeakable Adams".

He is a partner of one of Australia's most successful advertising agencies, Monahan Dayman Adams.

His film credits include "Hearts and Minds" (a pioneering documentary on Vietnam, made with Bruce Petty), "Jack and Jill: A Postscript", the first Australian film to win the major prize at an international film festival, "The Naked Bunyip", "The Adventures of Barry McKenzie" (Australia's first "new wave" success which went on to establish box office records in London), "Don's Party", "The Getting of Wisdom", and the animated feature "Grendel Grendel Grendel".

Phillip is now Managing Director of Adams-Packer Film Productions.

Ron Brown

Ron Brown, born Melbourne in 1927, graduated B.Sc. and M.Sc. from Melbourne University and Ph.D. from London University. He held lecturing positions at both universities before being appointed Professor of Chemistry at Monash in 1959.

In 1965 he was elected a Fellow of the Australian Academy of Science and has been a member of the Council of the Academy and Vice-President of Physical Sciences. He is Chairman of the National Committee for Chemistry and a member of the Sub-Committee on Chemical Education.

His current research interests cover theoretical chemistry, spectroscopy, galactochemistry and life in space; and he retains an interest in an earlier devotion — to badminton.

Ron Clarke

Ron Clarke, born in Melbourne in 1937, captained the Australian team at the Tokyo Olympiad in 1964.

Over a decade-and-a-half in competitive athletics, he set 36 Australian and 18 World track records in all distances from 2 miles to the 1-hour run, earning him 6 times the title Victorian Athlete of the Year. He won a bronze medal in Tokyo and silvers at 3 Commonwealth Games, being voted World Sportsman of the Year by the B.B.C. in 1965, and in 1966 by the French Institute of Sport.

He now runs Ron Clarke Sports, a division of I.M.I. Australia Operations P/L. A vocal advocate for the "Life. Be in it" campaign, he is a member of the Sports Council of Victoria and helps run the annual Melbourne to Frankston marathon.

He is the author of six well-selling books on athletics, and since 1966 has written a weekly column for The Age.

In 1966 Ron Clarke was made M.B.E. for his services to sport.

Neil Douglas

Neil Douglas, born 1911, has lived with his wife Abbie in the Victorian bush for many years at Kangaroo Ground, 40 kilometres from Melbourne. His mud-brick home is basically self-sufficient. He grows his own food and makes his own clothes.

He is a cultural activist who's much involved in the society from which he stands somewhat apart. At the age of 15 he initiated debate leading to the formation of the Country Fire Authority: half-a-century later he is still advocating many conservation issues, particularly those which would restrict damage to the bush he loves so much.

"By confronting the bush in all its beauty and wildness", Neil Douglas says, "we confront ourselves. And that is the basis of any real, living culture".

Barry Humphries

Barry Humphries, author, actor, song writer, artist, was born in Melbourne in 1934. Apart from his other work in theatre, television and films, Mr. Humphries has written and performed eight one-man shows since the early 1960's, the most recent of which is "An Evening's Intercourse with Barry Humphries".

Mr. Humphries has been entertaining his fellow Australians for over 20 years,

although his contribution to the theatre has only been officially recognized in the United Kingdom where he won the Society of West End Theatre Managements Award for the best comedy performance in 1979. In 1980 the British Association of Television and Film Arts awarded him two nominations for television comedy.

A section of Mr. Humphries' theatre writings from 1956 to 1981 has just been published in Britain and Australia under the title of "A Nice Night's Entertainment."

He is married with three children.

Sir Laurence Muir

Laurie (Laurence Macdonald) Muir, born 1925, was one of Australia's leading sharebrokers until his retirement in 1980.

He is a member of the Victoria Law Foundation, and was for many years Senior Partner in Potter Partners, on the Stock Exchange.

Sir Laurence was knighted in the Queen's Birthday Honours list of 1981, after serving the Victorian — and Australian — community for 4 decades. His posts have included directorships of the ANZ Bank, ACI, Wormald International and Commercial Union Assurance; chairmanship of the Canberra Development Board; and extensive work in many fields of medical service — with the Alfred Hospital, the Baker Institute of Medical Research, the Microsurgery Foundation, and the Royal Flying Doctor Service.

Olivia Newton-John

Born in Cambridge, England, Olivia spent her childhood in Melbourne, where her mother still lives. At 15, she won her first talent quest, which earned her a trip to England and a recording contract with Festival International. Her second single, "Banks of the Ohio", won her an English Silver Disc and an Australian Gold Disc; she won her first Grammy in 1973.

Olivia made her motion picture debut in "Grease", the biggest grossing musical of all time. Then came "Xanadu", one of the most lavish film fantasies of the '80's.

In spite of her "superstar" status, Olivia has managed to keep a steady balance in her life. She has settled at

Malibu, near Los Angeles in California, with her two cats, eight dogs and seven horses; and one of her greatest priorities today is her involvement with animals.

Sir Gustav Nossal

Gustav Nossal was born in Bad Ischl, Austria, in 1931, and came to Australia with his family in 1939. His research career has been primarily at the Walter and Eliza Hall Institute, of which he became Director in 1965. He is also Professor of Medical Biology at the University of Melbourne.

Professor Nossal's research is in fundamental immunology, in which field he has written three books and 270 scientific articles. He is also interested in the interface between science and society, as evidenced by his fourth, more general book "Medical Science and Human Goals", his membership of the Australian Science and Technology Council, and six years on the Council of the Australian Academy of Science. His work in the field of international health is carried out in collaboration with the World Health Organization, to which he has been a key consultant for 15 years. Sir Gustav Nossal was knighted in 1977.

Rennie Ellis

Photographer/journalist/writer Rennie Ellis was born in Melbourne in 1940. He now runs his own photographic agency, Scoopix. There are Ellis pictures — vignettes of Australian life, particularly in sub-cultures — in the National Gallery of Victoria, the Biblioteque Nationale in Paris, and in the Phillip Morris collection, Australian National Gallery, Canberra.

He won the Australian award in 1976 from the United Nations Conference on Human Settlements for a set of photographs exploring the theme: "Problems of people living together".

His books include "Australian Graffiti", "King's Cross, Sydney", and "Australia", published in Switzerland in 4 languages — but not in English! He has illustrated a successful book for children, "Ketut lives in Bali", and is working on another which has 30 different Australians expressing their views in both text and pictures on living in this country.

Robert Gray

Robert Gray was born on April 25, 1951, at the Queen Victoria Hospital, within earshot of the military bands of Melbourne's Anzac Day march parading down Swanston Street. He joined *The Age* as a cadet photographer, before heading off to work for some years in Queensland, Hong Kong and Canada. He has won Action Photograph of the Year awards from both the Victorian Football League and the Victorian Cricket Association, joining the honours list in the Tavern at the M.C.G.

He is principally a public relations photographer, working for corporate clients, and specializing in reportage for many company magazines.

Ian McKenzie

Ian McKenzie was born in Melbourne in 1939. He started learning his trade with Arthur Dickinson, then Mark Strizic, specializing in architectural and industrial photography. "There was little formal training available in Victoria when I started in photography", Ian says. "Now there's a good deal. I spent 2 years starting up one course at Prahran College of Advanced Education, but teaching isn't practice: I wanted to get back to the trade."

Ian has run his own studio for the last decade, developing what he describes as an "illustrative" style in commercial photography. "I'm interested in portraying a firm's *capacity* to produce rather than *what* they produce", he says.

He has been both Victorian and Federal President of the Institute of Australian Photography, and is one of the handful of professionals awarded by his peers the title of Master of Photography.

Paul Olson

Paul Olson, born Queenscliff, Victoria, in 1935, developed an early interest in film-making and graphics. He spent 4 years in Indonesia in the early '60's developing courses in printing and graphic arts under the auspices of the Colombo Plan, and writing 3 school textbooks, "which seem to be still in use".

Returning to Australia he spent several years working in advertising,

then opened his own photographic studio, specialising in advertising and audio-visual production. Portfolios of his photographs have earned numerous awards, including 2 Ilford national contests, and a Pentax International prize.

He lives in a large, overgrown bush block in Melbourne's eastern suburbs, playing "indifferent piano" in modern jazz idiom, and being "continually disappointed" by Australian politics. Much of his enthusiasm and most of his energy now go into a much less devious activity: bicycle racing.

Ron Ryan

Irish-born Ron Ryan arrived in Melbourne in Olympic year, 1956, at the age of 11. He was educated in Fine Arts at the Prahran and Royal Melbourne Institutes of Technology and at Melbourne University. He has since produced both words and pictures for most communications media in Australia.

A keen conservationist, Ron has written articles for Australian Walkabout and overseas wildlife magazines, and won a Hasselblad Masters Award in the demanding field of wildlife photography.

Ron currently directs 3 major agencies from his Elwood studio: Ron Ryan Studios; the Photographic Agency of Australia, an extensive visual library; and the Historical Photographic Agency.

Peter Thomson

At 24, Peter Thomson is one of the youngest photographers to have achieved success in Australia. He went into advertising photography at 17, working with Brandt, Imhoff and Street; cumulatively they were influential in developing Thomson's now graphic style.

The Thomson style has been seen in national and international campaigns for clients as varied as BHP, Telecom, SAAB, Heinz, Kodak, Phillips, and a recent 3-month Asian assignment for American Express. He has often worked with Barry Humphries on posters and books. Like Humphries, he has an interest in art glass, painting and bronze sculpture by artists of the early nineteen hundreds. Peter Thomson's future projects include documentary and commercial film making.

Facts and figures

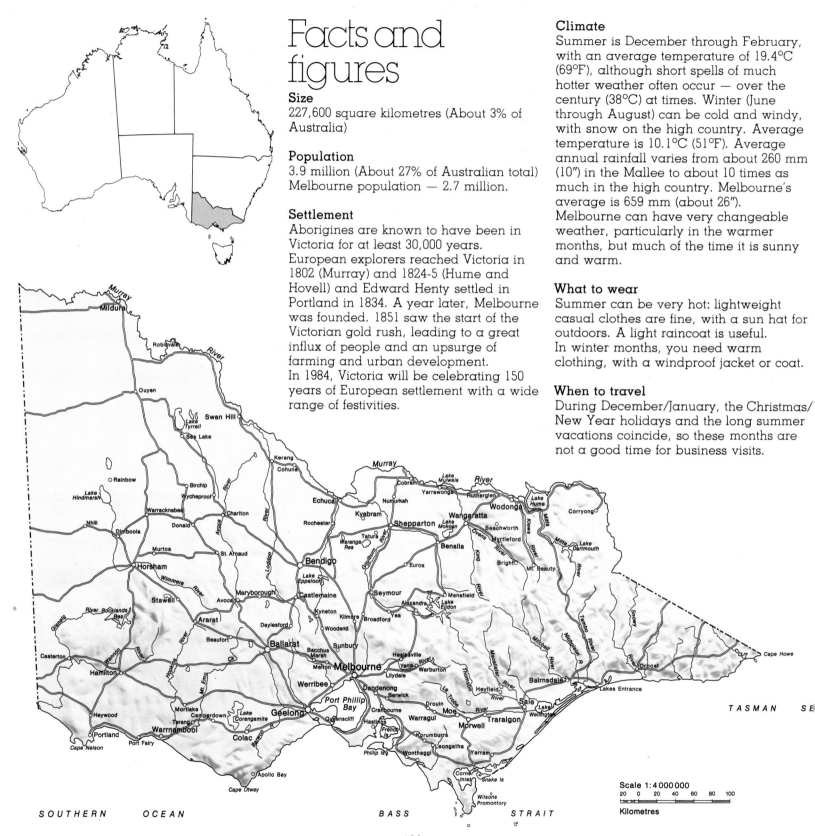

Size
227,600 square kilometres (About 3% of Australia)

Population
3.9 million (About 27% of Australian total)
Melbourne population — 2.7 million.

Settlement
Aborigines are known to have been in Victoria for at least 30,000 years. European explorers reached Victoria in 1802 (Murray) and 1824-5 (Hume and Hovell) and Edward Henty settled in Portland in 1834. A year later, Melbourne was founded. 1851 saw the start of the Victorian gold rush, leading to a great influx of people and an upsurge of farming and urban development.
In 1984, Victoria will be celebrating 150 years of European settlement with a wide range of festivities.

Climate
Summer is December through February, with an average temperature of 19.4°C (69°F), although short spells of much hotter weather often occur — over the century (38°C) at times. Winter (June through August) can be cold and windy, with snow on the high country. Average temperature is 10.1°C (51°F). Average annual rainfall varies from about 260 mm (10") in the Mallee to about 10 times as much in the high country. Melbourne's average is 659 mm (about 26").
Melbourne can have very changeable weather, particularly in the warmer months, but much of the time it is sunny and warm.

What to wear
Summer can be very hot: lightweight casual clothes are fine, with a sun hat for outdoors. A light raincoat is useful.
In winter months, you need warm clothing, with a windproof jacket or coat.

When to travel
During December/January, the Christmas/New Year holidays and the long summer vacations coincide, so these months are not a good time for business visits.

Grollo Fountain, officially inaugurated by Princess Alexandra in October 1980, reflected in the mirrors of Centennial Hall. The Hall extends display space in the Royal Exhibition Building, built in 1880 and home of both Australia's first Federal Parliament (from 1901 to 1927), and to the forty-two nation Commonwealth Heads of Government Meeting in 1981.

Highland music alfresco is one of a dozen musical and dramatic activities encouraged by the FEIP-people; Free Entertainment In Parks, enlivening summer since 1972, with shows ranging from teddy-bear rallies to brass band competitions. The fun continues in the winter, too, with weekly concerts in the Melbourne Town Hall.

Where to find out more

In Victoria, contact:
Publicity Unit,
Department of the Premier,
7th Floor,
49 Spring Street,
Melbourne, 3000
Telephone: (03) 651 3666
Telex: 32636

Victorian Government Travel Authority
230 Collins Street,
Melbourne, 3000
Telephone: (03) 602 9444
Telex: 30868
(Offices also in Ballarat, Bendigo,
Geelong, Mildura)

Melbourne Tourism Authority
80 Collins Street,
Melbourne, 3000
Telephone: (03) 654 2288
Telex: 32708

Victorian Economic Development
Corporation
A.N.Z. Tower,
55 Collins Street,
Melbourne, 3000
Telephone: (03) 654 1944
Telex: 30089 (VICDEV)

for Overseas, contact:
Agent-General for Victoria,
Victoria House,
Melbourne Place,
The Strand,
London, WC2B 4LG
Telephone: (01) 836 2656
Telex: 5121813

Commissioner for the Government of
Victoria in Japan,
Suite 304,
Tokyo Chamber of Commerce and
Industry Building,
3-2-2 Marunouchi,
Chiyoda-Ku,
Tokyo, 100. Japan.
Telephone: (03) 213 3061
Telex: 222 2567 (VICGOV J)

Commissioner for the Government of
Victoria,
The Paramount Plaza,
3550 Wilshire Boulevard,
Los Angeles, Calif., 90010.
U.S.A.
Telephone: (213) 387 3111
Telex: 324171 (VICECONDV LSA)

Victorian Government Travel Authority
Quay Tower,
29 Customs Street West,
Auckland, New Zealand
Telephone: 794 566
Telex: 21007

Or these offices of the Victorian Economic
Development Corporation
Bush House,
Strand,
London WC2B 4PA, England.
Telephone: (01) 836 0301
Telex: 21813 (YARRA G)

27-33 Champs-Elysees,
75008 Paris, France.
Telephone: (010 331) 723 4446
Telex: 280530 (VOXALE)

Bauernwagnerstrasse 1,
D-8 Munich 17, West Germany.
Telephone: (010 49 98) 755 4800
Telex: 522565 (WILDE D)

Corso Venezía, 2A
20121 Milano. Italy.
Telephone: (020 392) 79 8746
Telex: 314227 (PROFIT I)

Sydney Morrell & Co. Inc.,
152 East 78th Street,
New York. N.Y. 10021. U.S.A.
Telephone: (0101 212) 734 9159
Telex: 62396 (INTRPRES)